# LORE AND LEGENDS
# OF BASEBALL

## Books by the Same Author

FROM MOSES TO EINSTEIN

JEWS FIGHT TOO

GREAT AMERICAN SPORTS HUMOR

# *Lore and Legends*
## OF BASEBALL

### BY MAC DAVIS

ILLUSTRATED BY REYNOLD C. POLLACK

LANTERN PRESS INC., *Publishers*
257 FOURTH AVENUE, NEW YORK 10

Library of Congress Catalog Card Number: 53-5541

PUBLISHED SIMULTANEOUSLY IN CANADA BY
GEORGE J. MC LEOD, LIMITED, TORONTO, ONTARIO
MANUFACTURED IN THE UNITED STATES OF AMERICA

*To Florence and Nancy*

a couple of my loyal rooters
—in and out of season.

For Americans, there is no other game in the world like baseball. The national pastime is rooted deep in their hearts. It has become a way of life and something of a religion, generating the pure essence of joy. Baseball has become part of our national character, part of our culture, and part of our faith.

It is also democracy at work, for the game reduces people from all walks of life to a common denominator. Once a baseball game is on, everybody wants to get into the act.

The romance, the glamour, the color, the thrills, the drama, and the laughter of the game flow from generation to generation, inundating the corridors of memory with folklore.

Spread across the pages of this book are some of the fascinating tales, fantastic legends, colorful anecdotes, and little-known bits of humor and lore of the game.

The characters and situations in this book are not imaginary. Any resemblance to actual persons and places is not accidental. Everything did happen, if you can believe the truth as documented in dusty record books, preserved in the capricious memories of dugout historians, and recorded in the nostalgic chatter of baseball's old guard who trade in diamond fact, legend, lore, and myth.

MAC DAVIS

# CONTENTS

**LORE AND LEGENDS**

**OF BASEBALL** ☞

## INCREDIBLE—
## BUT IT HAPPENED

☛ **A FORTUNE FOR A PEBBLE**

Almost from the day old Abner Doubleday invented the game of baseball, the "bad bounce" has plagued all infielders. A pebble on a field has been the cause of many a freak hop which, in turn, has been the difference between victory and defeat.

A tiny pebble once decided a world-series championship. It happened years ago in the classic between the New York Giants and the Washington Senators. In the twelfth inning of the final game of that series, a ball was hit at Freddy Lindstrom, the Giants' star third baseman. Just as he set himself to field it, the ball struck a pebble, bounced over the third baseman's head, and allowed the winning run to come in, which decided the championship.

A pebble on the infield has actually changed the course of a man's life. There is one such strange tale in baseball lore.

Away back in 1905, William Griffiths was the first baseman of a club in Salt Lake City called "The Rhyolites." He was a mediocre busher, earning a meager salary.

One afternoon the home team played its bitter rival, "The Beattys." On first base was William Griffiths.

.3

In a late inning of the game, a batter hit a grounder toward him. Griffiths set himself to field that ball, when suddenly it hit a pebble on the field and sailed over his head.

With disgust, he walked over to the spot where the ball had taken the bad hop to pick up the stone. Just as he was about to throw the pebble away, something about it caught his eye, so he slipped it into his pocket.

No sooner was the game over than William Griffiths rushed back to his hotel room and carefully examined the little pebble he had found on the field. There was no doubt about it—that pebble was a gold nugget!

That night, secretly, first baseman Griffiths returned to the deserted baseball park. By the light of a lantern he spent hours digging in the soil, searching for other such golden pebbles. When he accumulated a bucketful of stones, he returned to his room. In the morning he had all the rocks assayed, and he discovered that they were worth more than $1,000 to the ton.

Then the ingenious bush-league first baseman contacted some friends who helped him raise the necessary cash, and, quietly and without any fanfare, he purchased the ball park.

Once this was done, William Griffiths turned that bush-league ball park into a mine, which, naturally enough, he named "First Base."

Before long, the mine yielded a fortune in gold, and the former bush-league first baseman became a millionaire.

## ☞ MAN OF PITCHING GLORY

The first pitcher in baseball history to hurl a no-hitter was Joseph E. Borden.

He was one of the game's most shadowy and tragic figures.

Joseph E. Borden came out of nowhere to achieve fame. In 1875 he was hired to play with Philadelphia of the National Association. One sunny afternoon he set down the Chicago batters without a hit or a run. It was the first no-hit game in baseball history!

In the beginning, Borden seemed to be present wherever baseball history was made. On April 22, 1876, the hope of an organized baseball circuit became a reality when the first National League game was played in Philadelphia. An overflow crowd of 3,000 fans jammed the ball park to see Philadelphia play Boston in that historic contest. On the mound for "bean-towners" was Joseph E. Borden, now hurling against his old teammates. Borden added to his fame as he took the contest and thus became the first pitcher to win a game in the National League.

However, Borden was not yet done with diamond glory. That baseball season of 1876 was but a month old when he pitched the second no-hit game in the annals of baseball, this time against Cincinnati.

The fame of Joe Borden spread far and wide. Wherever he went, people flocked to admire him. He became the first popular star of the game. Then, at the height of his success as baseball's greatest pitcher, his arm went lame. Borden couldn't win another game. He was useless to the Boston club. He tumbled from the heights, and finished the season he had so magnificently begun in the humble and obscure capacity of groundskeeper at the Boston ball park!

After that baseball year, Borden vanished. Nothing more was heard of the pitcher who had hurled the first no-hit game. Then one day, he was found toiling in a factory in Philadelphia. Ironically, he was earning a meager livelihood—stitching baseballs.

When his identity was established, Borden disappeared again. Nothing more was heard of him until his death at the age of thirty-five. Even in death, he made headlines, for he was drowned in the historic Johnstown flood of 1889, a national disaster that cost 2,000 lives.

## ☛ HIS FINAL RESTING PLACE

On the day in 1875 when Joseph E. Borden pitched the first no-hitter in baseball, his catcher was Lewis Brown.

Borden and Brown formed the most famous battery in the game. The story of Borden's receiver is as strange as his own.

Lewis "Blower" Brown was a powerful man, rugged and tough. To impress his teammates and rival players, he would often boast of his fistic ability.

As the legend goes, he became so impressed by his two-fisted prowess that he challenged Joe Goss, the bareknuckle heavyweight champion of the world. Goss, however, dismissed the ballplayer's challenge with such contempt that "Blower" Brown became the laughingstock of the baseball world. Because of that humiliation, the famous catcher developed a bitter hatred for Joe Goss.

For several years Brown remained the greatest catcher in the game. Then, at the height of his fame, his throwing arm suddenly went lame and he was forced to quit baseball. He found himself a job as bouncer in a Boston saloon. The drinking place was owned by the widow of Joe Goss—the man Brown had hated for years!

Only a few months before his batterymate, Borden, was to be killed in the historic Johnstown flood, Lewis Brown, only thirty-three, became ill and died, whereupon the widow of Joe Goss, in a sentimental and unusual gesture, buried him in the same grave with her departed pugilist husband!

No baseball player in history ever found a stranger final resting place than catcher Lewis "Blower" Brown.

### ☞ TALE OF NINE TOWNS

Baseball fame is fickle and anything but lasting. Many great stars who once blazed across the baseball heavens have been completely forgotten. All memory of them has faded to a handful of lines found only in dusty record books. But some baseball heroes have had their names perpetuated in strange and curious fashion.

There are many ways in which heroes of the national pastime have been honored. The immortal stars of the game dwell in Baseball's Hall of Fame at historic Cooperstown, with their images shaped in statues, and their diamond deeds recorded on plaques of bronze. Some have had books written about them; others have had Hollywood make motion pictures of their lives and baseball times, for all the world to see. Some have had streets, race horses, buildings, and even candy named after them. But the most unique honor ever accorded any baseball players, past or present, belongs to nine men of the Chicago White Sox team of long ago.

The batting order of that ancient ball club, name by name, read: Miller, Admire, Allen, Bushong, Rapp, Helmick, Wisley, Delevan, Comiskey. In their day, those were nine great stars, and they made diamond history. They were so popular that the officials of the old Missouri Pacific Railroad decided to record their fame with a decidedly unusual tribute.

That is why, today, travelers on the Missouri Pacific Railroad, on the main line between Kansas City and Denver, pass nine whistlestops—nine little towns called Miller, Admire, Allen, Bushong, Rapp, Helmick, Wisley, Delevan, and Comiskey!

## ☞ ME AND MY PAL

Some years before the turn of the century, there was a well-known leaguer named Cliff Carroll. He played with Pittsburgh. He had an inseparable friend who roomed with him and traveled around the league with him, day in and day out. One morning Carroll's friend died. Cliff was grief-stricken. So the Pittsburgh club actually staged a funeral in its ball park, and buried Cliff Carroll's friend under home plate.

Strangely enough, Cliff Carroll's pal, buried under home plate, in a funeral staged in a National League ball park, was a pet monkey.

## ☞ THEY WRAPPED HER FAME IN TIN FOIL

A long time ago, the Philadelphia National League team had a first baseman named Sid Farrar. Salaries for big-league ballplayers were low in those days, so Sid just about managed to get by on his small income.

The Phillies' first baseman had a little daughter, and he often brought her to the park to watch him play. His teammates fell in love with the pretty little girl and adopted her as their mascot.

As Sid Farrar's daughter grew older, the first baseman discovered that she had a good voice, so he ar-

ranged to give her a musical education. But teachers cost money, more than Sid Farrar could earn playing ball. He began to fret and worry.

One day his teammates found him rummaging through the stands after a game, picking up all the scraps of tin foil he could find. Sid Farrar was collecting tin foil and selling it, to earn a few extra dollars.

His teammates decided to help him. After every game played, the whole club searched the stands. They sold the tin foil, and the money went for voice lessons for Sid Farrar's daughter.

When the fans learned about Sid's struggle, they wanted to help also. They too collected tin foil, and before long, bales of it were shipped to him weekly.

There is a happy ending to this strange story: That Philadelphia first baseman's daughter grew up to become America's most famous opera singer, the darling of two continents, and perhaps the most fabulous star the famed Metropolitan Opera has ever had! She was the unforgettable prima donna known and loved throughout the world as Geraldine Farrar.

## THE OUTFIELDER WHO BECAME A HEALER

Once there was a famous major-league outfielder who led a million souls to salvation.

William Ashley Sunday was born in a log cabin in Iowa and was reared in an orphan asylum. At fifteen, so that he could get a free education, he found himself a job in a school. Each morning, hours before dawn, he lighted fourteen stoves. He kept fourteen fires going all the day, swept and polished the floors, and kept up with his studies. Surprisingly enough, Sunday also found time for a little baseball. He made something of a local reputation.

Before he was twenty-one he was up in the big leagues, playing for the Chicago White Sox. He was one of the speediest outfielders in the history of the game—the first ballplayer in history to circle the bases in less than 14 seconds. In the field he was a ball hawk; at bat he was a terror. Before the turn of the century, he was one of the highest-paid men in the game.

Famous star that he was, William Sunday, off the baseball field, was a wild character. His escapades were many, and he could "bend an elbow" with the best. His manager, the famed Pop Anson, had his hands full trying to keep his outfielder in line.

One night, after starring for five years with the Sox, Sunday went into a saloon with some of his teammates. Soon, he and his pals were drunk. Across the street, a company of men and women came marching along. They were singing gospel hymns. Sunday listened for a while, then suddenly stood up and said, "I'm finished with this life. Boys, we've come to the parting of the ways. I'm going into the service of God!"

His teammates laughed at him and mocked him. But the next day the baseball world was rocked by a sensational announcement. Billy Sunday, one of the most famous outfielders in the game, had quit the major leagues, at the height of his glory, to become a preacher. And he gave up a salary of $3,500 a season, big money in those days, to work for the Y.M.C.A. at $83 a month.

Billy Sunday became the most colorful and most famous evangelist in the world, and the most popular preacher in the history of the Christian pulpit. For thirty-five years the ex-big-league ballplayer roamed up and down the land, furiously preaching the gospel of God, and about one hundred million people flocked to hear his messages of sin and salvation. More than one million souls were personally led down the sawdust trail to redemption by this baseball outfielder who gave up fame and fortune as a major-league star—to turn evangelist!

### ☛ HIS DEBUT WAS HIS FAREWELL APPEARANCE

A strange finish to a major-league debut was the lot of a ballplayer named Harry Heitman.

In 1918 he became the "boy wonder" of the Brooklyn Dodgers' spring training camp. A great future was predicted for him as a major-league pitcher.

For his debut in the big leagues, he faced the St. Louis Cardinals.

The first batter singled. The next one tripled. The third man doubled, and the fourth batter hit a home run.

At this point, the patient Brooklyn manager finally gave up on the rookie pitcher and waved him off the mound. At the signal to leave, Harry Heitman stood on the hill—dumfounded. He seemed to be unable to accept the horrifying thought that his debut as a major leaguer had ended in such humiliation. But when he saw a relief pitcher swagger to the hill, he realized at last that "his finest hour" had turned into a heartbreaking moment of failure. Rookie Harry Heitman tossed away his glove, walked into the clubhouse, dressed, left the ball park, went to a recruiting station, enlisted in the Navy, and never again returned to pitch in the big leagues.

### ☛ $150,000 FOR A STOLEN BASE

One of the game's all-time "greats" was the famous "Peerless Leader" Frank Chance, first baseman and manager of the pennant-winning Chicago Cubs of old.

It is a well-known fact, substantiated by record books, that Chance was a remarkable hitter, a fine first baseman, and one of the best managers in major-league history. But that he was also one of the great base stealers is a story all its own.

In his baseball prime, Frank Chance was a huge man, perhaps the most powerful who ever appeared on a big-league diamond. Yet he was sufficiently fast of foot to steal as many as 67 bases in one season, and 57 in another! His base running was so daring and so remarkable that he once earned $150,000 for just one stolen base.

One summer's afternoon, the Chicago Cubs were playing Cincinnati. In the stands sat the Cubs' owner attentively watching his players in action. In a late inning, with one out, up to bat came Chance, and he promptly hit a single. On the next pitch he stole second. Needing a run to win that close game, Chance signaled the next Chicago batter to lay down a bunt, hoping to advance himself to third. Even before that bunt was laid down, Frank Chance began to run. He turned third, and, to the shocked amazement of the Cincinnati team, he continued his dash until he slid safely across the plate, scoring from second base on a bunt.

The owner of the Chicago club was so thrilled by that exhibition of base running, which he called the greatest play that he had ever seen, that, immediately after the game, he called Frank Chance into his office and gave him a tenth interest in the Chicago team for $10,000. He even loaned him the money to pay for that one-tenth share. Some years later, when Frank Chance sold his one-tenth of the Chicago club, he received $150,000 for it.

☛    **ROW YOUR BOAT**

When the amazing Chicago White Sox, "Hitless Wonders" of 1906, took the pennant and went on to win the baseball championship of the world, their success went to Hiram Connibear's head. An illiterate tough-and-rough tobacco-chewing guy, he was the trainer of the team. Hiram Connibear demanded a raise in pay of $200 more per season. He never got it. Instead he was fired. So Connibear found himself a new job. Oddly, it was a job at the University of Washington—as a rowing coach. The old ex-baseball trainer had never even seen a rowing shell!

Nevertheless, Connibear laboriously began to read and digest books on rowing, as he experimented with the technique of the sport. In time, he invented a method of oarsmanship that became famed as the "Connibear stroke." With that stroke, his Washington crews became the greatest in the sport, and Hiram Connibear became the most famous coach in the entire history of rowing.

### ☛ DUCKPINS FOR YOU

Nobody really knows who invented bowling, for it is said that the game originated almost two thousand years ago in Italy. But if you have ever bowled "duckpins," you may be interested in the story of how they originated.

It all began shortly before 1900. In those days, the city of Baltimore, with its legendary Orioles, was the baseball capital of the world.

The Orioles had a pasty-faced, brawling little Irishman playing third base for them—John J. McGraw. His best pal was the catcher of the team, a jolly ballplayer named Wilbert Robinson.

One day, the teammates decided to go into business, as a side line. They opened a tavern with bowling alleys, and called it "The Diamond."

To "The Diamond" flocked the sporting gentry of the day, some to the bar, others to spend time on the bowling alleys, playing tenpins. At the time, it was the best-known version of the ancient game of bowls which the Dutch had imported to America.

The proprietors of the tavern found the venture most profitable. McGraw was especially interested in the bowling alleys. He supervised them with a loving and shrewd eye, always trying to think up ways of making the place more popular.

It became the custom of John McGraw to give the worn-out big maple pins to boys playing in a near-by park. However, always a man with an eye for an extra dollar, McGraw decided one day that it might be advisable not to throw away the used pins but to have this marred equipment shaved down in size so that the pins would still be usable.

McGraw carried the big pins to a woodworker and ordered him to cut them down. This done, he placed ten of them on an alley, anxious to see how the keglers would greet the innovation. The cut-down bowling pins aroused the interest of the surprised bowlers, for they found them much harder to hit. Soon, most of the keglers who came to the tavern wanted to bowl with the diminutive pins.

Thereupon, McGraw and Robinson ordered a carpenter to make more little ones out of big ones. Soon after, McGraw and his partner went duck hunting.

While firing away at the wild fowl, Wilbert Robinson turned to McGraw and said, "John, don't the ducks scatter in every direction just like our little bowling pins do when somebody hits them?"

And McGraw happily shouted: "Robbie, you've just given me an idea. Let's call the new invention "duckpins!"

Thus, the name was born.

The years passed. In time, the two tavern keepers were to thrill millions with their major-league feats —Robinson as the unforgettable manager of the Brooklyn Dodgers, and John McGraw as perhaps the greatest big-league manager in all baseball history.

That much is well known by all, but hardly anyone knows that John J. McGraw, the fabulous "Little Napoleon of Baseball," was also the man who originated the bowling game now played by millions of people the world over—the game now known as "duckpins."

## LIGHT THE CANDLES

In 1889 St. Louis and Brooklyn were locked in a torrid race for the flag, and came down to the final game of the season in a tie. Late in the game that was to decide the championship of the league, St. Louis was leading 4 to 2, and victory seemed certain. Suddenly, the sky clouded up, and a fog enveloped the playing field. Immediately, the pennant-hungry St. Louis players set up a loud clamor to have the game called on account of darkness, for it would have made them the league champions then and there. But the lone umpire officiating seemed to be in no hurry. He ordered play to continue. Whereupon, Arlie Latham, the St. Louis third baseman, decided to force the issue with the stub-

born arbiter. He ordered the bat boy to bring him a dozen large candles. When the youngster returned with them, the clowning Latham lined up the twelve candles in front of the St. Louis dugout and lit them. The fans howled with laughter at the stunt, but that hint had no effect on the umpire. He simply walked over and blew out the candles. However, when he resumed his post on the playing field, the St. Louis third baseman sneaked back and relit all the candles. Again the umpire blew them out. Again Arlie Latham relit them. Finally the umpire became roaring angry, walked up to the stands, and, in a voice heard throughout the ball park, announced that the game was forfeited to Brooklyn. Thus St. Louis, even though ahead in the score and apparently a sure winner, lost the game and the pennant because of twelve candles.

## 🖙 THAT'S HOW IMMORTALS ARE BORN

He started as a left-handed pitcher in the bush leagues. He started six times and lost six times. One afternoon, after he had lost by a score of 22 to 4, the manager told him to pack up and get out. The disheartened moundsman gave up pitching. He became an outfielder.

One day a baseball scout for the Pittsburgh Pirates saw him play, and he was impressed. He decided to sign this unknown outfielder for the Pirates. However, when the scout phoned his club owner for permission to give the boy a contract, Barney Dreyfuss refused to grant such permission for he discovered that the ballplayer smoked cigarettes.

Time passed, and the Boston Red Sox bought that outfielder for $400. At the time, he was with Little Rock. However, that season the Red Sox failed to take home their $400 purchase, for the club had trained at Little Rock, and he was left there in lieu of ground rent. That was how the Red Sox paid off for the use of a ball park for spring-training practice.

Eventually, that outfielder arrived in Boston and the big leagues, and for the next twenty-two years he won fame as one of the great center fielders of all time.

Who was he? Tris Speaker!

## 🖙 A DRAMA BEHIND LOCKED DOORS

In his school days, Jackie Robinson was one of the greatest of all college athletes. He was an all-American football player at U.C.L.A. He was one of the best track men of modern times and a broad-jump champion. He was also a star basketball player, a fine tennis player, and a good two-fisted fighter. However, he yearned most for baseball fame. Although he was an unusual ballplayer, his opportunities for diamond glory were limited to baseball's side roads and back alleys. For his skin was black. Never before had a Negro played in the big leagues.

On August 29, 1945, a somewhat bewildered

Robinson was ushered into the private office of Branch Rickey, then owner of the Brooklyn Dodgers. Only the young Negro ballplayer and the veteran baseball man who had spent most of his life in the game were in the room. Behind locked doors these two men changed the course of baseball.

"I know you can play ball," said Branch Rickey to Jackie Robinson. "My scouts tell me that. But what I want to know is, have you the guts to play the game no matter what happens?"

"I haven't had it easy in any sport," Robinson answered grimly. "They've been throwing at my head ever since I started."

Branch Rickey's voice rose. He shouted: "But it was never like it may be now!"

Then suddenly he rushed at Robinson and deliberately bumped him hard.

"Make believe I'm a player in the big leagues, and we're in a tight game. I'm coming into second base and you're there playing the bag. I purposely knock you down because I'm white and you're black. When I get up, I call you ugly names. What do you do then, boy? Tell me, Jackie, what will you do then?"

"I won't be afraid to fight back!" replied Robinson.

"Yes, I know you can fight," said Rickey. "But are you a ballplayer with guts enough not to fight back when they insult you, push you, spike you, and punch you? That's what I want to know. What will you do then, Jackie?"

Robinson's lips trembled before he answered, and then in his soft voice he gently replied, "Mister Rickey, I've got two cheeks to turn to all who abuse me. Is that what you want me to do, to be a major-league ballplayer? I'm not afraid to try."

Branch Rickey nodded his head as he wiped the sweat from his forehead, and a warm smile spread across his face. He was not only a business leader but a man of heart, courage, and purpose, too. Then and there he knew that his search was over. He had found in Jackie Robinson not only the first Negro ballplayer good enough and courageous enough to defy the unwritten Jim Crow law, but a baseball gold mine as well.

That was how the color line was wiped out in organized baseball, when Jackie Robinson became a pioneer—the first Negro to play in the big leagues and go on to fame as one of the most remarkable players in the game's history.

### SIXTY-SIX INCHES OF BALLPLAYER

Phil Rizzuto's success story is a tale to bolster the courage of all little men everywhere.

Brooklyn-born, when Phil Rizzuto finished school he received an invitation to a mass tryout with the Brooklyn Dodgers. The Dodger manager took one look at the sawed-off runt and bluntly told the boy to go home and forget about becoming a major-league player. That manager's name was Casey Stengel.

In time, little Phil Rizzuto came to the Yankees. To sign him, it cost the rich New York club exactly 15 cents—10 cents for telephone calls, and 5 cents for a cup of coffee when the boy arrived for the signing. When he first reported to the Yankees, he was so small and puny-looking that the watchman refused to let him enter the dressing room. He thought that Rizzuto was seeking autographs of the Yankee stars.

Surprisingly enough, little Phil Rizzuto, only 66 inches high, became one of the great shortstops of the game. He sparked the Yankees to 6 pennants and 4 successive world championships—for a Yankee manager named Casey Stengel—the same Stengel who once had rejected him as a player because he was too small.

## ☞ THE BALLPLAYER WHO WAS KICKED OUT OF TOWN

Many years ago there was a boy named Frank Lausche who yearned to become a ballplayer. He was good, too, but somehow he found the going rough. Still, he had his hopes for better baseball days to come.

Frank Lausche plied his talents as an outfielder on the sand lots and in the bush-league ball parks of Ohio. He traveled with a team called the Cleveland All-Stars.

It happened that the Dillonvale Indians, the pride

and joy of the baseball-mad town of Dillonvale, Ohio, had an open date on their schedule. Their boss and manager, a man named John Olszeski, booked the Cleveland All-Stars for a double-header. Lausche, captain of the Cleveland All-Stars, sold the manager of the Dillonvale team a "bill of goods" to the effect that his crew of crackerjack ballplayers would give the Dillonvale Indians and the fans a run for their money.

The double-header was advertised far and wide. On the big day, the town turned out en masse to see the twin bill.

It was a sad day for Frank Lausche and his team-mates. The first game was a fiasco, as the Dillonvale Indians crushed them under a barrage of hits, runs, and fancy fielding.

But if the first game was bad, the second game of that double-header was worse. It was a massacre, as the Dillonvale Indians made about 50 runs. Frank Lausche single-handed tried to stem the rolling tide flowing over home plate, but it was all in vain.

The Dillonvale fans rioted. Lausche and his frightened teammates were lucky to escape from the ball park alive!

Shortly after playing those two games, Frank returned to see the manager of the Dillonvale Indians, and he demanded the few dollars he had been promised for himself and his teammates. But the Dillonvale manager refused to pay off. After much wrangling, Lausche finally received his money. However, the manager warned him to leave fast before a mob of angry fans rode him out of town—on a rail.

So, baseball player Frank Lausche left that Ohio town in disgrace. But, strangely enough, in time he became one of the most famous men in the state— Governor of Ohio!

🖙   **FABLE OF A MURDER**

In the sordid annals of crime, there is record of a murder. It happened many years ago. This is how that bloody tale unfolds.

One night long ago, a saloonkeeper was about to close up when two tough-looking men entered and demanded his money. As he reluctantly turned to empty his cash drawer, he snatched at a baseball bat he kept hidden under the bar. But the thugs were too fast for him. They wrested the club from his hands and viciously beat him to death—with his own bat.

It is strange that this grim story of an unsolved murder should be closely linked with the romance of baseball. For, ironically enough, the murdered saloonkeeper was the father of a son, who in later years, won imperishable fame and a fortune of $2,000,000—with a baseball bat.

He grew up to become known over the world as the mightiest home-run slugger of all time—Babe Ruth.

### ☛  YOURS—ABSOLUTELY FREE

Socking home runs in large numbers has been the ambition of many baseball sluggers. But in more than a hundred years, only 6 men have hit 4 home runs in a single game—Bobby Lowe and Ed Delahanty of the old days, Chuck Klein and Lou Gehrig of the baseball '30's, and Pat Seerey and Gil Hodges of recent big-league vintage.

However, the home-run slugger who holds a unique distinction is a ballplayer known to the records as Jay Justin "Nig" Clarke. He was once the big-league batterymate of Cleveland's immortal pitcher, Addie Joss, and he was one of those who pioneered shin guards for catchers.

When Clarke was just a rookie catcher with the Corsicana baseball club of the Texas League, he came to bat one afternoon for his first lick. He hit a home run. On his second appearance at the plate, he again hit a home run. His third time up, he hit another, as he did on his fourth time at bat.

Therefter, each time Nig Clarke came to the batter's box the stands were in an uproar as the fans demanded just one more circuit blow. When Nig made his fifth try, a rich Texas cattleman shouted: "Hit another home run, Clarke, and I'll give you fifty dollars!" Nig socked one out of the park—his fifth straight homer of the afternoon. The next time he was at bat, a rival cattle baron rushed out on the field waving a hundred-dollar bill and offered it to the rookie catcher if he would hit still another. So, Nig Clarke obliged, and hit his sixth consecutive round-tripper.

All in all, in that amazing baseball game, Clarke came to bat eight times—and he hit eight straight home runs.

Afterward, the fans surrounded Nig and showered him with money. The hat was passed, and $500 was collected. Added to that, some of his frenzied admirers, who were local merchants, gave him dozens of suits, shirts, neckties, underwear, socks, and shoes as his reward for hitting eight straight home runs in eight consecutive times at bat!

## ☞  EDUCATION OF A ROOKIE

Many years ago, an unknown rookie came to the Detroit Tigers to play the outfield. He was a cocky, pink-cheeked boy from the South, with star dust in his eyes. However, his early days with the Detroit club were bitter ones. The veterans hazed him mercilessly. They broke his bats, tore his uniform, and cut up his baseball shoes, and his own roommate actually locked him out at night more than once.

The rookie took it all in silence. For those were rugged days in baseball, and every veteran's hand was raised against a new player. Many promising recruits were ruined before they had really started because of the treatment they received from hostile veterans. This rookie, too, seemed to be fading fast as a potential big-leaguer because of the cruel hazing.

One night, he took a walk with Nig Clarke. For a few moments the two stumped along in silence, when suddenly the unhappy rookie burst out: "I don't know what to do anymore. Those big apes are driving me crazy. Even my own roommate is against me. What am I going to do?"

The catcher looked at the unhappy and worried kid. He barked at him: "Don't come crying to me! If you're a ballplayer and want to stick in the big leagues, you can't be soft. Get in there and fight for your rights."

The rookie took his advice. The next morning he had made an important decision that was to change the course of his life. Within the next month, he had five pitched battles in the Detroit dressing room with his own teammates, and six fist fights on the field with rival players. As the baseball days passed by, that once meek boy became the most vicious ballplayer in the big leagues. With fist, with tongue, and with spikes he cut down any player who stood in his way. He became the most feared player in baseball—and perhaps the greatest. As a result, his career in the major leagues lasted twenty-four years, and he created almost 100 individual records. He is the only player to make more than 4,000 hits. He won the batting championship of the American League 12 times and wound up with an incredible lifetime batting average of .367.

In Baseball's Hall of Fame he is immortalized as the "Georgia Peach," Ty Cobb.


☞  **THE CYCLE OF TWO**

Of all athletes in the world of sports, baseball players are the most superstitious. One reason for this may well be found in the weird tale of a shortstop once known to fame as Ray Chapman.

He was the only ballplayer ever killed in a major-league baseball game.

In his heyday Ray Chapman was the star shortstop of the Cleveland Indians. For a decade he was one of the best in the game. However, he was a ballplayer obsessed by an odd compulsion. He was superstitious about the number 2.

Ray Chapman never entered a place, first. He always made sure he was preceded by someone. He tried to transact all his private business on the second day of the month. When it was his turn to hit, he would always come to the plate swinging two bats. Before he faced the pitcher, he would always tap home plate with his foot—twice. Naturally, he batted second in the Cleveland line-up.

On August 16, 1920, Chapman, sparking the Cleveland Indians to an American League pennant, played out his superstition to the end.

For on that day, in that major-league baseball game played against the New York Yankees, shortstop Ray Chapman, with the count 2 and 2, hit 2 two-baggers. Twice that afternoon, with the count 2 and 2, he was hit by a pitched ball. At the close of that baseball day, the figures in the daily box score beside Ray Chapman's name read thus:

Times at bat—2          Hits—2
Runs scored—2          Stolen bases—2

In the field, it was:

Put-outs—2
Assists—2
Errors—2

On his last time at bat, in the seventh inning, Ray Chapman was struck by a pitched ball for the second time that afternoon. It completed the cycle of 2 for him, for the ball fractured his skull and, soon after, the great shortstop was dead.

It was 2 minutes after 2 o'clock the next morning when Ray Chapman closed his eyes forever.

### ☛ TAKE ME OUT TO THE BALL GAME

The most popular song ever written about baseball is the familiar, "Take Me Out to the Ball Game." The story behind this song is a curiosity in the lore and legends of the national pastime.

Around the turn of the century, the American vaudeville stage featured a popular song-and-dance man known as Jack Norworth. Old-timers steeped in the history of the theater remember him as the stage partner of the glamorous musical-comedy star, Nora Bayes.

In his day, Jack Norworth also wrote tunes. He composed many of the ballads he sang before enthusiastic theater audiences.

It was a glorious era in baseball. The game featured such diamond immortals as Tinker, Evers, and Chance, Christy Mathewson, Napoleon Lajoie, Wee Willie Keeler, and other famous and unforgettable players. But Jack Norworth had no interest in baseball and its heroes. The stage was his sole passion.

However, Norworth was a shrewd showman. He realized the importance of the game in American life. He decided to capitalize on the game's popularity and add a baseball song to his act. One morning in 1906, Jack Norworth wrote a song about baseball. That night from the stage of a theater, with some trepidation, he introduced and sang it. The name of the ballad was "Take Me Out to the Ball Game." When he finished, the audience literally went wild, making him sing it again and again.

The song was a hit. It took the country by storm, and became America's most popular tune as people, young and old, sang, hummed, and whistled it. For it was a gay song that expressed all the excitement and color of baseball. Before long, the national pastime adopted it.

Down through the years, "Take Me Out to the Ball Game" has retained its popularity. It has remained the theme song of the game of baseball.

The strangest part of the story is that the man who wrote baseball's greatest song had never seen a ball game in his life. Even after he composed the song, Jack Norworth had so little interest in the game that he waited thirty-four years before he saw his first big-league contest.

### ☞ CASEY AT THE BAT

The most popular poem about baseball is that old classic: "Casey at the Bat."

How often have you heard these lines?

Oh, somewhere in this favored land, the sun is shining
   bright,
The band is playing somewhere, and somewhere hearts
   are light,
And somewhere men are laughing and somewhere children shout,
But there is no joy in Mudville—mighty Casey has
   struck out.

A young man named Ernest L. Thayer wrote it. This is the story.

At Harvard University, young Thayer yearned for fame as a baseball player, but he wasn't good enough to make the team. Upon his graduation from college, he went West and became a reporter for the *San Francisco Examiner*. He could not forget his love for the game of baseball. Although he sadly realized that baseball glory was not for him, he became an enthusiastic fan. He was a faithful follower of a mighty slugger of that day, John Patrick Cahill, the star of a San Francisco professional club.

One day, when Thayer was at the ball park rooting for his hero, Cahill stepped up to the plate with two men out in the ninth, two on base, and one run needed to tie the score. The crowd roared for Cahill to come through. Majestically, Cahill stood at the plate and contemptuously let two strikes go by. Then on the next pitch, he took a tremendous cut at the ball—and missed. The mighty slugger, John Patrick Cahill, had struck out—and the game was lost.

Young Thayer, suffering keenly from the disappointment of that defeat and the downfall of his hero, returned to his newspaper office and wrote "Casey at the Bat." For his poem, he used the name of Casey only because he hadn't the heart to humiliate his friend Cahill.

The poem was printed by the *San Francisco Examiner* on June 3, 1888. It created a sensation and quickly became a national favorite. Ever since, actors have delighted audiences in almost every American city with recitations of "Casey at the Bat." To this day, the poem written by a frustrated ballplayer is universally accepted as a classic—the most popular poem ever written about the game of baseball.

## 👉 FRANK MERRIWELL IN PERSON

Louis Sockalexis was the first full-blooded Indian ever to play in the majors. It was shortly before the turn of the century, when he arrived in Ohio to play for the club then known as the Cleveland Spiders.

Sockalexis was an athlete to stir the imagination! He was handsome; he was graceful; he was fast. He was an outfielder, and when it came to throwing a baseball, no one ever had a stronger arm than Sockalexis. Before each game, he used to give exhibitions. He would stand in deep center field and hurl the ball to the catcher, without a bounce, for strikes!

Louis Sockalexis played barely three seasons with Cleveland, but in that brief span he established himself as one of the greatest outfielders of all time!

No Cleveland ball hawk ever caused a greater sensation than this gentle, soft-spoken Indian. So famous did he become, that the Cleveland club changed its nickname from the Cleveland Spiders to the Cleveland Indians!

Sensational as was the rise of Sockalexis as a star, his sudden end as a baseball hero was shocking. His downfall began during a gay party. Sockalexis always drank milk, but at this party some of his teammates, in a playful mood, taunted him into taking his first drink of hard liquor. That prank destroyed Sockalexis as a ballplayer. He developed a taste for alcohol and lost all control of himself. Before long, he

drifted out of the big leagues, and professional baseball would have no part of this once-amazing Indian.
Sockalexis became a street beggar, shuffling along,
dressed in shabby clothes, asking for pennies. He
died while still young.

Ironically, although Louis Sockalexis had such an
unhappy and speedy end as a ballplayer, for many
years now he has been a shining hero to millions of
American boys. For this gentle Indian was such a
fantastic athlete that he inspired an unknown writer
named Gilbert Patten to create the character of
Frank Merriwell, who has thrilled countless boys
with his feats of athletic daring. Yes, it was Sockalexis, who served as the model for fiction's fabled
hero.

### ☛ OVER A FOOLISH QUARREL

About 1900, the Chicago Cubs startled the
baseball world when they started two rookies in their
infield. Both were little men—mere boys of 20.
Johnny Evers was installed at second. Joe Tinker
was placed at short. The two rookies became pals,
as well as two-thirds of the most fabulous double-
play combination of all time—"Tinker-to-Evers-to-
Chance"! Johnny Evers and Joe Tinker paced the
Chicago Cubs to 4 pennants and 2 world-series
championships in five years. Then one day in 1908,
Joe Tinker and Johnny Evers had a quarrel. It happened because Evers took a hack to the ball park, and

drove off without offering his pal a ride. The two friends stopped talking to each other, and although they played side by side, and remained the same wonderful double-play combination, they never spoke a word to each other. For some twenty-five years thereafter, Johnny Evers and Joe Tinker nursed their grudge in silence and bitterness.

### ☞ THE FEMALE OF THE SPECIES

The baseball institution known as "Ladies' Day" is almost as old as the game.

In the season of 1897, the Washington Senators decided to make a bid for female patronage. The club owner figured a free invitation to the gals would be good publicity and attract a few hundred curious women.

But when the gates opened that September afternoon, thousands of ladies appeared and jammed into the Washington park. The object of their interest was George "Winnie" Mercer, a particularly handsome pitcher who was scheduled to hurl for Washington that day.

Early in that game, Mercer began to find fault with the umpire's decisions on balls and strikes. The stands, to a woman, sided with "Winnie" Mercer against the umpire, Bill Carpenter by name.

In the fifth inning "Winnie" made an elaborate ceremony of giving the umpire a pair of eyeglasses. The ladies shrieked with delight. But umpire Carpenter was not amused, and without hesitation, he ordered the handsome pitcher to leave the field.

The women in the stands leaped to their feet and screamed imprecations at Carpenter.

When the game was over, thousands of infuriated females poured from the stands, shouting threats at the umpire. Carpenter, who never before had quailed before the fury of fan or player, became frightened as he hastened to cover. But before he could gain the safety of the Washington clubhouse, several women mauled him and tore his clothes. Once inside, Carpenter demanded that the Washington players protect him. The doors were bolted and the window shutters closed as a hail of stones and bricks crashed against the structure. Many of the enraged women used their parasols to beat against the shutters. Some even found clubs with which they tried to break down the door. While this was going on, another horde vented their rage on the ball park. Seats were ripped out, windows broken, railings bent. The police were called, but the "ladies" remained in the ball park until dark, still waiting for the umpire. To save his life, the poor arbiter had to be smuggled out. At last, the mob dispersed, but many years were to pass before the Washington club dared stage another "Ladies' Day."

## ☞ LADIES OF THE DIAMOND

When Babe Didrickson was the greatest all-round athlete of her sex, she actually pitched one inning against a major-league team in an exhibition game. Whether the ballplayers rigged it or not, it is a matter of record that the incredible Babe struck out two of the three major-leaguers she faced.

But for stamina, durability, length of service, and

devotion to the game of baseball, no player ever equaled the amazing record of a lady ballplayer named Mae Arbaugh.

Playing under the name of "Carrie Nation," Mae Arbaugh was a professional ballplayer who toured the country with the famed Bloomer Girls, an amazing team that played all comers, male or female. Mae was the star attraction in every game. She could slug the ball with the best of them, fielded brilliantly, and stole bases with speed, grace, and ease. She could play almost every position with equal ability. Thousands flocked to ball parks all over the country to see her.

Mae Arbaugh participated in 4,000 baseball games, more than any other major-leaguer, and her baseball career covered all of thirty-three years!

### ☞ LOVE ME—LOVE MY GIRL

Years ago, a gangling eighteen-year-old boy came into the office of the Chattanooga baseball club, and asked for a pass for his girl friend. It was almost game time, and the Chattanooga manager was too busy fretting about his team's chances of winning to be bothering with the request of a rookie infielder who evidently was trying to impress his girl.

"Don't bother me!" curtly snapped the Chattanooga manager. "Let her buy a ticket for the game."

The shy rookie argued with the busy manager until the annoyed pilot roared at him: "Why, you fresh busher! Just who in blazes do you think you are?"

"I'm Marty Marion, and I'm going home!" said the rookie as he stormed out of the room.

The refusal of a free ticket cost Chattanooga a ballplayer. But more important, it cost its parent club, the Washington Senators, the greatest shortstop of modern times—Marty Marion, "Mr. Shortstop" himself.

### ☛ FROM HERE TO ETERNITY—AND BACK

The story of Bruce Campbell is unique in baseball lore.

Campbell first played big-league baseball with the Chicago White Sox. It didn't take too long for him to establish himself as a star outfielder, and, subsequently, he played with five other major-league clubs.

One afternoon when he was with Cleveland, Bruce Campbell began to suffer a fierce headache. He didn't complain, and finished the game. But that night his headache became worse. He went to see a doctor. The ballplayer heard the bad news. He had become a victim of the dread disease—spinal meningitis! Soon paralysis began to creep over his body. His life was slowly ebbing away, and the doctors gave up all hope. Campbell's mother was constantly at her son's bedside, hoping and praying. Then came the crisis. Bruce tried to whisper something to his mother, but no sound came from his lips. His eyes closed, his hands dropped, and all was still. Hurriedly, the doctor came, felt the ballplayer's pulse, listened to his heartbeat, and then shook his head as he turned to the grief-stricken mother and said: "Your son is dead!" Several minutes later, as the doctor began to write his report, Campbell's mother suddenly screamed. Hysterically, she insisted that she had noticed her dead son flicker an eyelid. Feverishly, the doctor began to work over the ballplayer whom he had officially pronounced dead. A miracle came to pass. Bruce Campbell's life was saved.

Thirty days later he was playing baseball again in the major leagues.

## ☞ THE FISHERMAN'S SON

Years ago, a slender fourteen-year-old boy played with the San Francisco Junior High School baseball team. That lad stood out from his teammates because he was the only one on the team who didn't wear a uniform. The boy couldn't afford it. His father was a humble Italian fisherman with eight mouths to feed, and there was no money for such things.

One day, the coach of the high-school team said to the boy:

"Kid, put your mind to it. You might become good enough to be paid for playing ball. Why, some day you might make the San Francisco Seals."

"Who, me?" asked the startled boy, and then he sadly shook his head and mumbled, "Questo É Matto." Luckily, the coach didn't understand Italian, for what that boy had said was, "This guy is crazy."

To every San Francisco boy, the Seals were the greatest baseball team in the world, and how could a poor fisherman's son hope, even in his wildest dreams, to play baseball with those famous heroes?

Shortly afterward, the boy was asked to play on a team in the Industrial League. He was paid for it, too. The fisherman's son was confused. His mind was divided: whether to play baseball for money or stick to his schoolbooks for a while longer. His oldest brother solved that problem quickly. He told him to stay in school or he'd punch his ears off.

Although you could take the boy out of baseball, you could not take baseball out of the boy.

A couple of years later, fate in the guise of a baseball scout, Spike Hennessey, caught the fisherman's son peering through a hole in the fence of the Seals' ball park.

"Listen, boy," said the Seals' scout, "I'll get you into the ball park so you can see the games. Maybe, if you can play, I'll fix it so you can work out mornings with the team."

"G'wan, stop kidding me!" retorted the boy, "They wouldn't let me do that."

They did. And before long, they signed up that fisherman's son to play with the San Francisco Seals. He was eighteen then, and in his first season the fisherman's son created a record with his bat. He hit safely in 61 consecutive games.

Three years later, he was in the big leagues as an outfielder with the New York Yankees.

Such was the beginning of the legend of Joe DiMaggio—the highest paid ballplayer in history, an outfielder so great he earned $100,000 a season.

## FIVE BROTHERS FOR BASEBALL

The most famous "brother act" in baseball history was that of the Delahanty clan. Five brothers made the big leagues—Jim, Joe, Tom, Frank, and Ed. The most famous was the eldest, big Ed Delahanty. It was he who carved the family name deep in baseball lore, with a fantastic legend of success and failure.

While the other Delahanty brothers were hardworking, serious players, Ed was a wild Irishman with incredible talent and a taste for excitement. He was a first baseman. Once in Chicago, he made 5 hits in five times at bat, with 4 home runs. Of all the mighty sluggers who played in the major leagues, he stands alone for one achievement. Only he led both major leagues in batting. He accomplished that remarkable feat by hitting .408 for the Philadelphia Nationals in 1899; and in 1902 he won the batting championship of the American League, while playing for the Washington Senators, hitting .376.

Ed Delahanty played sixteen years in the big time,

and he ended the Delahanty "brother act" in a pathetic way. One night, high in spirits, the wild Irishman created a disturbance in a Pullman railroad car. He was ejected from the train at Fort Erie, Ontario, at the Canadian end of the International Bridge. By that time, he was a half-crazed man, and, in a weeping rage, Delahanty set out after the departing train. He threw aside a night watchman who tried to stop him, and started across the bridge. Delahanty refused to heed a warning that the draw was open. He stumbled off into the darkness and plunged into the roaring waters of the Niagara. Days later, they found Ed Delahanty's mangled body, as a shocked nation read the news of the sudden passing of the greatest baseball player of his era. It was a macabre finish for a titan of the game, as well as the end of the greatest "brother act" in baseball history.

## ☛ DOWN TO THE BOTTOM THEY WENT

The Cleveland team of 1899 suffered the most discouraging string of defeats in big-league history. That Cleveland club was the worst club in major-league annals—a team so incompetent that it won only 20 games in an entire season, was forced to finish with an undertaker for a manager, and finally quit the league entirely.

In 1899 Cleveland started the season with high hopes for glory.

Cleveland won the opening game, but promptly lost the next 7. From then on that Cleveland team just lost and lost. Players began to desert the club, and, before long, even its manager quit in disgust. Australian-born Joe Quinn reluctantly took over the pilot reins. By trade, he was an undertaker, and he was more interested in his gloomy business than in rallying his dejected players to occasional victory.

In August of that season, the hapless Clevelanders ran up a string of 24 consecutive defeats. Finally, they managed to win a contest, but almost immediately started another losing streak of 16 straight. The club wound up a disastrous season, losing 40 of its last 41 games.

On the last day, Cleveland's undertaker-manager supplied the final comic touch. For that morning he was accosted by a total stranger who informed him that he was the cigar clerk in the hotel lobby, and that he had always yearned to pitch. Influenced by a gift of a box of cigars, the Cleveland manager permitted that hotel clerk to pitch the final game for his team. With that farce, the 1899 Cleveland team concluded a season in which it won only 20 games and lost a staggering total of 134—winding up 80 games behind the pennant winner of the year.

Cleveland never again played in the National League. Out of sheer embarrassment, it quit the senior group and joined the newly formed American League.

## ☞ HE OBJECTED TO A HIT

He was somewhat on the runty side, fresh out of the sleepy little town of Harrah, in Oklahoma, when he first swaggered out on a field to play as a major-leaguer.

He was a rookie outfielder for the Pittsburgh Pirates. On his first day in the big leagues he was frightened, and to soothe his jangled nerves he squawked at the plate umpire's decisions—just to show what a tough ballplayer he was.

When he managed to get a hit and reached first base, Bill Klem, who was officiating there, said to him: "Young man, you look like a good ballplayer to me—but you're starting out on the wrong foot by arguing with umpires. You won't get far fighting us. Relax, son, and take it easy, and you'll last a long time in the majors."

The rookie took the famous umpire's advice. Soon enough, the baseball world sang the praises of little Paul Waner, dubbed "Big Poison."

Although his eyes were so weak that when he was at bat he could hardly see the outfield fences, he nevertheless starred in the major leagues for seventeen years. He won fame not only as one of baseball's great outfielders but as one of the most incredible batters of all time. He was an artist with his bat, and he acted with the grace and dignity of one.

On the afternoon of June 17, 1942, Paul Waner was with the Boston Braves, and he was almost at the end of his career as a big-league star. His hit total had reached 2,999. Everyone in the ball park was pulling for him to register just one more hit and enter the superexclusive 3,000-hit club. For only six stars in baseball history were members of that exclusive group.

The fading outfielder came up to bat, picked out a good pitch, and bombarded it into the field to the left of second base. The rival shortstop barely managed to get his glove on a piece of the ball, but he could not field it in time for the put-out.

As Waner reached first, all eyes seemed to turn for a ruling toward the official scorer in the press box. For a moment the scorer hesitated, and then he signaled it to be a hit. The stands broke into cheers. Umpire Beans Reardon raced over to first base with the prize ball in his hand, and he offered it to Paul Waner as a souvenir of a historic event—the moment when he had made his three-thousandth hit. But Waner refused to accept the ball. He was standing on first base, hands cupped to his mouth as he shouted to the scorer, "Don't give me a hit! I don't want a hit on that play. I won't take it!"

Paul Waner kicked up such a fuss about that dubious hit that he forced the official scorer to reverse himself and rule the play an error by the Cincinnati shortstop.

When that was done, Waner smiled with satisfaction and said, "I'm glad. I want my three-thousandth hit to be a clean one!"

There is a happy ending to this story for a few

days later Paul Waner hammered out a clean hit and
joined the 3,000-hit club. He wound up his major-
league career with a record of 3,152 hits. In 1951
that amazing little man ended his journey to glory
by being elected an immortal to Baseball's Hall of
Fame.

## 🖝 LITTLE BASEBALL SECRETS FROM THE
## WHITE HOUSE

One of the keenest players in the early days
of the game was Abraham Lincoln. The story is told
that when a committee came to his home to inform
him that he had been nominated for President of
the United States, Abraham Lincoln was in a field
playing ball. He made the committee members wait
on the side lines with the important news until he
had his turn at bat.

It was William Howard Taft who originated the
custom of a President of the United States throwing
out the first ball at the opening game of a major-
league season.

In his youth he was a catcher. So skilled a backstop
was Taft that, when only sixteen, the Cincinnati Red
Stockings offered him a contract for $800 a season.
However, his stern father forbade him to pursue the
career of a professional. So he gave up his dream of
baseball glory and grew up to become the twenty-
sixth President of the United States.

It was Benjamin Harrison, twenty-third President of the United States, who tagged the New York club of the National League with its nickname. One day the New York team visited the White House. As the ballplayers entered the audience room, the President gasped at the sight of all those six-footers and exclaimed: "My, they're giants."

Ever since then, the New York National League team has been known as the Giants.

Warren G. Harding was the best-informed of all presidential baseball fans. Before he became chief executive, he owned a professional team in Marion, Ohio. He was a keen judge of baseball talent. Some of the players he personally scouted and discovered made the grade in the majors.

Woodrow Wilson was perhaps the most ardent baseball fan among the Presidents. While a student at Princeton University, he made every effort but failed to make the varsity. However, his interest in baseball remained great for he became a very successful manager of the Princeton team.

Calvin Coolidge was one President of the United States who showed little enthusiasm for the game. It took much persuasion to get him to attend his first major-league opener and throw out the first ball. Until he did so, he had never held a baseball in his hand. Bored, he left in the third inning.

A man once refused an offer to become a professional, and it cost him his life. In his youth, he was so good a player that several clubs sought his services. But he rejected baseball and gave up the game. He turned to politics, and in time he reached the highest office that the American people had the power to bestow on any man—President of the

United States. The honor cost him his life, for he was assassinated. His name was William McKinley.

Herbert Hoover was a varsity shortstop at Stanford, and even after he won fame in public life he remained a fan. Unfortunately, it was destined for him to be the only President of the United States to suffer public humiliation at a baseball game. In the 1931 world series, President Hoover came to Shibe Park in Philadelphia to see the game between Philadelphia and St. Louis. At the time, the country was in the deep throes of a depression, and prohibition was the law of the land. No sooner had President Hoover entered the ball park, when thousands of people rose to their feet and booed him. Then they screamed: "We want beer!" That episode was the forerunner of a political upheaval that changed the history of the country. For soon after, Herbert Hoover was defeated for the Presidency of the United States by another baseball fan named Franklin Delano Roosevelt.

In his youth Franklin D. Roosevelt had such a great love for the game that when he failed to make his school nine, he became the team's water boy. No President of the United States ever threw out as many first balls in opening-day ceremonies as he did.

Years ago a boy lived in Missouri who yearned to become a ballplayer. But because of weak eyes, he had to wear glasses. The other lads of the town rarely gave him a chance to play in their games. However, he always pestered them for a chance to play. Mostly to be rid of him, the boy was made an umpire. That frustrated ballplayer became the President of the United States—Harry S. Truman.

**BASEBALL**
**IS A VERY FUNNY GAME**

There are stories in the lore of baseball to prove that Rube Waddell was the greatest left-handed pitcher of all time. In one season alone, he struck out 343 batters. Over a stretch of seven big-league seasons, he whiffed 1,801 hitters—still a major-league record. In his prime, he was a hurler of incredible stamina. In 1902 he pitched in every game of a six-game series against Detroit, and in the last one—in the last inning—he actually ordered his outfielders to come in and squat on the grass as he proceeded to strike out three batters to win the contest single-handed.

Rube was also one of the real loons of baseball. Once he wandered away from his team to sign up with a fire department, just so he could ride the engines. Time and again he missed ball games for a chance to lead a parade. During the height of one season, he disappeared for ten days and pitched for a sand-lot team because he wanted to have time to fish. Once he disappeared and was finally discovered posing in a show window as a clothing dummy. On another occasion, he was found wrestling live alligators for $2 a performance. He also jumped from a ferryboat when someone in jest shouted that a woman had fallen overboard. Before a mob of cheering spectators, he dived again and again into the chilly river to find a nonexistent body. Once, he jumped out of a two-story window to win a ten-dollar bet.

Rube Waddell never drew a pay check in his life. He would always receive an advance from the club secretary as needed, and the rest would be banked for him. Once, Rube Waddell requested $25 for a suit. He promptly bought himself an outfit for $13. The rest he kept for a good time. When he returned to his hotel room, he took off his old suit and went to the window to throw it out, on the premise that nobody needed more than one suit of clothes. His roommate, however, asked him for the suit, and Waddell gave it to him. A couple of days later, Rube's new suit was beginning to be soiled. He spotted his roommate wearing the old suit, now neatly cleaned and pressed.

"Those are nice clothes," said Waddell to his teammate. "Tell you what. I'll trade this new suit of mine which I only bought a couple of days ago for yours." So the deal was made, and Rube traded his new suit for the very one he had thrown away.

In 1913 Rube Waddell's team was in spring training at Hickman, Kentucky, on the banks of the Mississippi River. One afternoon while he was pitching, a fearful cry raced through the little ball park:

"The levee has broken!"

Panic seized the town. Men, women, and children ran for their lives to escape the raging floodwaters.

But Waddell didn't run away. He ripped off his shirt and, stripped to the waist, joined the company of other brave men who piled sandbags to stop the roaring flood on its path of destruction.

From midafternoon to almost three o'clock the next morning, Rube Waddell worked like a demon, standing in water to his waist. Finally, the flood was brought under control, and the little town was saved.

It was a worn and weary Rube who returned to his hotel room. He was shaking and shivering with cold, but he was happy.

Pitcher Rube Waddell was never the same after that day. Although a powerful man of unusual strength, he came down with a heavy cold and never quite recovered. He became a tragic victim of tuberculosis, and slowly wasted away.

He was only thirty-seven when the end came, but he joked to the last. Rube Waddell passed from this world in a manner befitting a clown—on April Fool's Day—April 1, 1914.

## ◀ HE ALMOST CAUGHT A GRAPEFRUIT

"Gabby" Street was one of the great catchers. He was the batterymate of that immortal pitcher, Walter Johnson. Yet Gabby Street's reputation rests primarily on a feat he once performed far from a baseball field. On such trifles often depend the glory of some of baseball's immortals.

One day during the 1908 season, Gabby Street

accepted a challenge to catch a baseball dropped from the top of the Washington Monument—a height of 555 feet. He did it!

That feat attracted world-wide attention. It became Gabby's ironic monument, for to his dying day, the trick catch outlived his fame as a great backstop.

For years thereafter, catchers young and old, famous and unknown, envious of Gabby's moment of glory, sought to win fame with trick catches, But no one was ever to achieve any measure of fame with a circus catch except Wilbert Robinson. His feat enriched baseball lore with one of its funniest stories.

In his youth, Wilbert Robinson had earned fame as a catcher for the Baltimore Orioles. Those were the days when the Orioles shaped baseball history as the game's greatest team. However, as the years went by, Wilbert Robinson became fat, round, and funny. He ended up as the eccentric manager of the Brooklyn Dodgers. Under his piloting, the Brooklyn club twice became a pennant winner but was known as the daffiest baseball team in the leagues.

One morning while the Brooklyn team was in spring training in Florida, a discussion arose among the players about great catchers. Before long, the unforgettable trick catch of Gabby Street was brought up. But Robinson scoffed at it. He stubbornly insisted that he would have equaled the stunt, and even now, old as he was, he was willing to show his players that he could catch a ball thrown from an even greater height.

One word led to another. Finally, Robinson was goaded into betting $100 that he could catch a baseball thrown from an airplane. It was agreed that Casey Stengel, then an outfielder with the Dodgers, was to go up in a rented plane and toss out a ball.

Came the moment for the great experiment. Robinson planted himself in the middle of the baseball field and waited for Stengel, in a plane overhead, to drop the ball. Round and round circled the airplane jockeying for position. Down on the ground, fat Wilbert Robinson craned his neck to follow it, frantically waddling around in circles.

Finally, the big moment arrived. Down came the

spherical object. Robinson set himself to snare it. However, unknown to him, it wasn't a ball that had been dropped from the plane. At the last moment, the clowning Casey Stengel had substituted a grapefruit for a baseball—just for a laugh.

That large sphere came down with tremendous speed, and it cracked poor unsuspecting Robinson with a resounding thud, broke, and squashed all over him. He almost drowned.

"Boys," he gasped, "I'd have caught that ball if there hadn't been a cloudburst just before I got my hands on it."

Only hours afterward did Wilbert Robinson discover that he had been the butt of a joke. He got so mad that he actually grabbed his hunting rifle and went gunning for Casey Stengel who, for days, wisely avoided the furious baseball manager.

## ☞ A BALLPLAYER MUST SLEEP

Many baseball seasons ago, Ossie Schreckengost and his roommate, Rube Waddell, formed one of the great batteries. The two were inseparable pals. To save additional expense for their club, as was the custom in those early days of baseball, they shared the same bed in their hotel room.

One season, catcher Schreckengost refused to sign his contract, which amazed Connie Mack since his catcher had clearly been satisfied with the salary offered. When pressed for an explanation, Schreckengost told his manager that he would only sign if a special clause were written into Waddell's contract. Manager Connie Mack thought this a touching bit of loyalty between two friends. However, to his sur-

prise he discovered that the clause which the catcher wanted in his roommate's contract was one forbidding Rube from eating animal crackers in bed!

Only when that was done, did catcher Schreckengost sign.

## ☞ BALLPLAYER, WHERE'S MY CHILD?

There was a time when the eccentric Babe Herman brought his little son to the ball park and placed him in a grandstand seat before the game started, so the child could watch his famous father play.

The mighty Herman had a big day—a couple of home runs, a triple, and a double in four times at bat. It was a happy Babe who rushed home and sat down at the dinner table, his face beaming with pride.

"Where's the boy?" asked his wife.

"What boy?" replied the bemused Babe. Then it suddenly dawned on him that he had forgotten his son. He rushed back to the ball park, and there he found the little boy sitting in the grandstand, all alone. Red-faced with embarrassment, the absent-minded Babe brought his son home.

## ☞ $300 FOR A HAIRCUT AND SHAVE

Casey Stengel holds a unique record as the only major-league manager who has won 4 consecutive pennants and 4 consecutive world-series championships in his first three years as pilot of the New York Yankees. He also has the odd distinction of being the only ballplayer in big-league history who ever paid $300 for a haircut and shave. It happened when he was an outfielder for John McGraw's New York Giants.

In those days, many of McGraw's best players were hard drinkers. The miracle manager copped 10 pennants during his reign, but it was a constant battle with the incorrigible elbow-benders who starred on his teams. Nothing so infuriated McGraw as the sight of a drunken ballplayer!

One afternoon before an important game, Mc-Graw assembled his players in the locker room and gave them an angry talk. The main object of his furious address was a star who had showed up in tipsy condition. John McGraw raved and ranted on the vices of drink. He had just reached the climax of his fury by plastering a stiff fine on the erring player, when suddenly the door swung open and into the locker room swaggered outfielder Casey Stengel. He was late, because he was fresh from the barber-shop where he had had the "complete works." His hair was cut and neatly plastered down, and his newly shaved face was liberally dosed with bay rum.

The smell of bay rum roused McGraw as a red flag does a bull. Furiously, he walked up to the sur-prised outfielder, sniffed him for a moment, and then angrily roared: "You, too? How dare you show up smelling like a saloon. You no good, drunken tramp—I'm fining you a hundred bucks!"

The shocked Casey Stengel, who was cold sober, found his voice. He roared back at McGraw: "You're out of your head, Mac—I didn't touch a drop—"

An even angrier McGraw retorted: "All right, Casey, and there's another hundred-dollar fine for lying to me!"

This time, Stengel really exploded. He shouted: "You're blind and you're crazy, Mac! I don't care what you say—"

McGraw hollered back: "And it'll cost you another hundred for insubordination!"

That ended all argument. Casey Stergel paid $300 for a haircut, a shave, and a liberal dose of bay rum.

## REMBRANDTS ON THE LOOSE

One day the St. Louis Cardinals were staying at the swanky Bellevue-Stratford hotel in Philadelphia. Bored with himself, Pepper Martin was wandering around backstairs in that stately hostelry when he came across a supply of painters' uniforms, pails, and brushes. A happy idea came to the ever-clowning Pepper. He persuaded two other celebrated eccentrics of the team, Dizzy and Daffy Dean, to join him. Whereupon, he and his assistants donned the painters' white togs and made for the main dining room with the buckets, brushes, and ladders. The room was crowded with diners. Into that elegant restaurant swaggered Pepper Martin, followed by his two helpers.

"C'mon folks," he yelled, "everybody scram. We gotta get these walls done. There's a banquet here in a coupla hours. Everybody beat it and never mind paying your checks—it's all on the house."

Before the horrified manager knew what had happened, most of the startled diners had left without paying their checks. It cost Pepper Martin's boss a couple of thousand dollars to square the complaint of the angry manager and save Pepper from going to jail.


### ☛ BATTER TO SEE HIM

One murky afternoon, Lefty Gomez was pitching against Bobby Feller. Feller's ball was blazing fast that day. In a late inning, Gomez, a notoriously weak hitter, came to bat. By that time it was so dark that Feller's fast ball was just a blur on its journey to home plate. As Gomez stepped into the batter's box, he took a match from his pocket, lit it, and held it over his head.

The umpire took it good-naturedly and asked, "Do you think that will help you see Feller's fast ball?"

"Who wants to see his fast ball?" quipped Gomez. "I just want to be sure Feller sees me!"


### ☛ IT WAS NO PICTURE ON THE WALL

A major-league baseball club was once kicked out of its spring training camp hotel because of a steak.

It happened years ago to Connie Mack and his Philadelphia Athletics. One evening after a hard practice session in the broiling sun, Ossie Schreckengost, the great but eccentric catcher for the A's, walked into the dining room and ordered a steak. Ossie tried to cut it but found it too tough. He went out, got a hammer and nails, and proceeded to nail that tough steak to the restaurant wall. The hotel management promptly kicked Connie Mack and all his ballplayers out of the hotel. It took almost the entire night for Connie to find another billet for his players so the team could continue with its spring training.

### ☛ A GAY TROUBADOUR

Baseball has had many jokesters, but none quite like Herman "Germany" Schaefer. He was a natural comedian.

During his seventeen years in the big leagues he was a second baseman, a first baseman, a third baseman, and a shortstop. He played with Detroit, Chicago, Washington, New York, and Cleveland, and wherever he went, he spread laughter.

He was with Detroit when, one balmy afternoon, the Tigers were playing the famous White Sox— the "Hitless Wonders" who had won the world series the previous year. A partisan Chicago crowd of some 20,000 was on hand rooting against the hated Tigers. Came the ninth inning, and with two out and a man on first, Detroit sent in "Germany" Schaefer—as a pinch hitter. The Tigers were a run behind. A deafening jeer greeted Schaefer as he swaggered to the plate. With a majestic sweep of his

hand, he silenced them, as he bellowed for all to hear: "Ladies and gentlemen, you are about to see Herman Schaefer, the world's greatest batsman, give you a personal demonstration of his hitting powers!"

The tough Chicago crowd gave him a rousing razzing, but, undaunted, the amazing clown belted the first pitch into the stands for a home run. He began to circle the bases, and slid into first as he roared: "At the quarter, Schaefer leads by a head!" Then he slid into second and shouted: "At the half, Schaefer leads by a length." He came into third and bellowed: "Schaefer leads by a mile!" Then he slid into home plate, slowly dusted himself off, turned to the stands, and bellowed: "This, ladies and gentlemen, concludes Herman Schaefer's performance for this afternoon. The world's greatest batter—thank you, one and all!"

"Germany" Schaefer could squeeze a laugh out of the most serious situations. Once, with the playing field a lake because of a pouring rain, Umpire Billy Evans refused to call a game. The Tigers were a half dozen runs behind. They had loafed in the hope that five innings would not be finished, and they would be saved from certain defeat. So, when it came time for Schaefer to take his turn at bat, he showed up at the plate in high wading boots and a rubber raincoat, with a bat in one hand, and an open umbrella and lighted lantern in the other. The roar that came from the stands so embarrassed the stubborn umpire that he retreated in confusion and called the game!

### ☞ WHAT WAS THERE TO SAY AFTER THAT?

There was the time when Casey Stengel was an outfielder with the Giants, and the New York club came to a small Southern town to play an exhibition game. That afternoon Casey was wonderful as a ballplayer. He hit three home runs, made sensational catches in the field, and even stole a couple of bases. However, he heard very few cheers, for only two dozen people turned out to see the game.

That night, the town council threw a banquet for the visiting Giants, and the dining room of the leading hotel was crowded with the most important people of the town. All came to pay tribute to the visiting major-leaguers. Then, Casey Stengel, the hero of the game was called upon to say a few words. He rose and said: "It's nice to see so many of you here tonight. But where in blazes were all you lazy bums this afternoon when you could have seen me play some real ball?"

### ☞ NO WONDER HE WAS A WANDERER

Bucky "Bobo" Newsom has been with more major-league teams than any other ballplayer in history. He pitched for ten clubs. Although only at times was he one of baseball's great moundsmen, he was *always* one of baseball's great clowns.

"Bobo" was fired from ball clubs for the strangest reasons. Once, some rabbits cost him a job with a major-league team. He sneaked a flock of live bunnies into his hotel room, and kept them there until they were discovered by a hysterical hotel manager. The rabbits had eaten up a brand-new sofa, and about six yards of rug. The angry hotel man threatened to evict the whole ball club, and he was only pacified when the clowning "Bobo" was given his walking papers.

## ☞ HERE COMES CHARLEY

There was once a ballplayer named Charley Faust. He was a big-league pitcher, yet he never pitched a single ball to a rival batter in a major-league game. And, curiously enough, he helped a team win a pennant and caused it to lose a world series.

One day, back in 1911, a homely, grinning farmer from Marion, Kansas, showed up uninvited at the New York Giants' camp. He said to the startled manager, John McGraw: "My name's Charley Faust. I'm a pitcher—come all the way from Kansas 'cause a fortune-teller told me that I wuz goin' to help the Giants win a pennant. So here I am."

It happened at the time that the Giants were in a bad slump, and McGraw was ready for any diversion. So McGraw said: "I've been waiting for you, Charley. Go into the clubhouse and get yourself a uniform. We need a pitcher like you."

They dressed Charley Faust in a real big-league outfit, and he took his place on the Giants' bench, waiting for the call to mound duty. It was all a stunt, strictly for laughs.

But with Charley Faust on the Giants' bench, the team suddenly came out of its slump and began to win. Although he couldn't pitch a lick, Faust made all the players feel good. But he began to tease McGraw for a chance to pitch. Annoyed, McGraw decided to end the joke. He left instructions to keep Charley Faust out of the clubhouse. Promptly, the Giants began to lose. The players grumbled, and they demanded that Charley be brought back. They even offered to pay his salary.

So, Charley Faust returned, and before all his players, the proud John McGraw apologized and said: "Charley, it was all a mistake. I want you to be a member of our team."

The pitching clown grinned and replied: "Sure, Mac, I'll stick around and help you win the pennant."

Thus, Charley Faust became a full-fledged pitcher for the 1911 Giants at a regular salary. But he never was given a chance to face a batter. Manager McGraw kept promising to send him in, but the day never arrived.

Meanwhile, the clown took over the Giants team. He showed the players how to slide, the pitchers how to throw, and the fielders how to play their positions. He became such an attraction that he received offers to appear in vaudeville for $250 a week. He went on the stage, but no sooner did he leave the Giants than the team fell into a slump and began to lose steadily. Charley Faust gave up his lucrative stage career and returned to the Giants' dugout. He proved such a good-luck charm that there were actually several attempts to kidnap him.

Charley Faust inspired the Giants to win the pennant. Came the world series, and the clown demanded that he finally be given his chance to pitch. McGraw curtly dismissed his request. So Charley Faust, hurt and disappointed, packed up and went home to Kansas. The Giants lost that series. Embittered at the discovery that he had been used only for laughs, Charley Faust never returned to the big time. Three years later, a gloomy, silent man, he died, still bitter at John McGraw and baseball.

### ☛ THE CLOWN WHO FORGOT TO LAUGH

In the good old days when laughter was the keynote of spring training, the Brooklyn Dodger camp was "headquarters" for eccentrics, clowns, and loony bushers.

The oddest character ever to hit a Dodger training camp was Pea Ridge Day, a hog caller from Arkansas. He was a powerful man who often startled the countryside with weird howls, mostly in the dead of the night. Pea Ridge Day looked as though he had the makings of a big-league pitcher, but he was too busy manufacturing laughs for the boys. He would bet his teammates that he could break a belt strapped around him, by merely huffing and puffing. And he did. One day, the players inveigled Pea Ridge into a big wager, and, unknown to him, they substituted a harness strap for an ordinary belt. Trying to win that bet, Pea Ridge Day collapsed with two broken ribs. That finished his boasting. He had a sorry end. In a gloomy mood, Pea Ridge took his own life.

### ☞ SIMPLICITY WAS HIS VIRTUE

After Yogi Berra had helped the New York Yankees win the baseball championship of the world, he came home to his native St. Louis to be guest of honor at a banquet. Showered with gifts, he sat listening to eulogies of himself. Finally came his turn to respond. Yogi grabbed the microphone and roared with simple honesty: "Ladies and gentlemen, I want to thank you all who made this occasion necessary!"

Berra was asked to be a speaker at a small-town banquet. Yogi was instructed to bow to the right and say, "Mr. Mayor"; then bow to the left and say, "Mr. Toastmaster"; then bow to the audience and say, "Honored guests, ladies, and gentlemen." But by that time, poor Yogi seemed bewildered with all the instructions for his proper deportment as an after-dinner speaker, for he scratched his head, puzzled, and naïvely asked: "But supposing the mayor is on my left—what do I do then?"

Once manager Stengel bawled Berra out for doing something wrong while at the plate. "Why don't you think when you're at bat?" angrily roared the manager.

And Yogi Berra replied in all simplicity: "I can't think and bat at the same time!"

## PROFILE OF AN ECCENTRIC

Chris Von Der Ahe, without doubt, was one of the more colorful major-league club owners. With his broad face, his bulbous nose, his whiskers, and his shining top hat, he was a character out of fiction. A German saloonkeeper who spoke with a heavy accent, he became the owner of the St. Louis Browns quite by accident. He knew nothing about baseball, but Chris Von Der Ahe lost no time in making his team the most talked about in the game. He turned his St. Louis ball park into a Coney Island, with brass bands, girl trumpeters, chute-the-chute slides, a race track, and beer gardens. His team traveled from hotel to ball park in open carriages pulled by fine horses, and Chris Von Der Ahe would lead his team on the field in parade formation. He named apartment houses he owned after the star players of his team. Even depositing the daily box-office receipts became a special ceremony. After every game the cash was carried to the bank in a wheelbarrow as owner Chris Von Der Ahe marched behind, armed with a rifle and flanked

by guards. He was so impressed with his own importance as a club owner that he had a life-sized statue of himself made and placed in his ball park for all to admire.

In victory or defeat, he spent with a lavish hand. In 1888 when his St. Louis Browns won the pennant, owner Chris Von Der Ahe really went overboard. He ordered champagne for the whole team, for the newspapermen, and for the loyal fans—for everybody! When his Browns departed for New York to play the Giants in the world series, Von Der Ahe hired a private railroad train for the trip, and for each of his players he bought a new wardrobe. In the big town, he threw a party that lasted for three days. Champagne flowed like water. That party was the most expensive baseball party ever staged, for it cost Chris $50,000!

Eccentric and comical as he was, nobody could get away with anything on Old Chris. He was not a fool! Once, he presented each of the players with a suit of clothes. All outfits were exact duplicates of the fancy and expensive suit the owner wore. The players were overjoyed by the gift. Later, to their embarrassment, they discovered why their owner had been so generous. Some of the men had been lax about training rules and Chris Von Der Ahe had figured out a most ingenious trap. He hired private detectives and instructed them to watch the popular saloons for customers who were wearing flamboyant suits "just like the one I wear." A number of the St. Louis players who were breaking the training rules were caught and fined.

However, the colorful, generous, and perhaps the most honorable of all club owners had an unhappy end. He fell on evil days. His championship teams collapsed, and he lost money. In 1898 his ball park burned to the ground, and Chris Von Der Ahe nearly went out of his mind with grief. He was swamped by lawsuits, deserted by his friends, and betrayed by the other league magnates who finally drove him out of baseball. He ended his days in poverty, and when he died, a brokenhearted man, his life-sized statue was placed over his grave.

### SINK OR SWIM

Cleveland's one-time pitcher, Stanley Coveleskie, was an ardent but somewhat eccentric fisherman. While pitching his way into the record book, he still pursued the angling sport, filling his hotel bathtub with live bait. Once he went rowing with the brilliant rookie shortstop, Joe Sewell. Stanley asked Joe if he could swim, and when the boy confessed he didn't know how, Coveleskie told him that now was the time to learn. So he picked Joe up and threw him overboard, leaving him struggling in the water as he rowed away. The joke almost turned into a tragedy, for Sewell nearly drowned before he was rescued.

## ☛ NO SILK SHIRTS FOR HIM

Arlie Latham was not only the first paid baseball coach in history, but he was also the first celebrated funmaker. During the twenty-six years he played pro ball, he was famed as the most talkative player in the game. It was he who originated "dugout jockeying" and the ribbing of opponents from the coaching box.

His salty tongue made him widely feared. Once, a rich fan made a unique offer to silence Latham. He guaranteed to outfit him with silk shirts and silk socks during his entire career if he could keep absolutely quiet through one complete game. Arlie jumped at the offer.

The next afternoon, his team was engaged in a tight battle. Latham suffered in silence through the early innings. He kept his tongue in leash and his lips buttoned. The game went into the ninth inning and Arlie still hadn't uttered a single word. Suddenly his team rallied and put the winning run on base. Up jumped Latham, rushed over to the stands where the rich fan sat, and screamed at him: "To hell with clothes! Who wants to wear silk shirts and silk socks anyway!" And he began to yell louder than ever before as he beseeched his teammates to win the game.

Clown that he was, Arlie Latham was so popular as a big-leaguer that when the initial round-the-world baseball trip was organized, he was the first man invited to play on the American team. And it was he who was given the honor of explaining the game of baseball to the King of England.

## ☞ THERE'S SOMETHING ABOUT A SOUTHPAW

Years ago, opinion was that Lefty Lee Grissom had the makings of real greatness as a pitcher, but he established himself as one of the wackiest ballplayers of all time.

A professor at the University of California first discovered Grissom as a pitcher. The teacher wrote a letter to a friend of his, who happened to be the fiery redhead of baseball, Larry MacPhail, then boss of the Cincinnati club. MacPhail signed Grissom and told him to report to Cincinnati's camp for rookies at Beckley, West Virginia.

The miners used to come to this park just to see Lefty Grissom throw. He would warm up about twelve times a day to thrill them with the speed of his fast ball.

One afternoon, Lefty pitched and won handily. But when the game was over, he remained standing on the mound, shaking everyone's hand. By the time he had greeted all his admirers, his teammates had left by bus. In spiked shoes and uniform, he had to trudge over five miles of country road to return to the hotel.

Once, after a winning game, he disappeared while still dressed in his uniform. That evening, he was found marching with a traveling minstrel show along Main Street. One day, his arm felt a little sore. Someone told him that one of baseball's greatest pitchers, Lefty Grove, had two teeth removed in an effort to restore his "dead arm." So Grissom rushed to a dentist and had four perfectly good teeth pulled. Often, after he pitched a good game for Cincinnati, he would go on a sit-down strike and demand a boost in salary.

His antics finally drove him from the big leagues.


### 🖎 A LITTLE RABBIT ON THE PROWL

There never was a shortstop quite like Walter "Rabbit" Maranville. He is one of the legendary heroes of baseball and one of its real humorists.

Although he broke his leg four times during his career, the mischievous little "Rabbit" remained in the big leagues almost a quarter of a century. He was forty-eight when he played his last game at shortstop in organized ball.

Once, while fully clothed, he actually swam the Charles River rather than walk across a bridge.

Another time, when his teammates locked him out of his hotel room, he climbed out on a narrow ledge to gain entrance by way of the window. The ledge on which the mad Rabbit walked was twenty-five stories above the street!

There were times when he swallowed live goldfish, just for the laughs, and kept pigeons in the closet of his hotel room. He used to travel with a parrot on one shoulder, and a monkey on the other.

The escapades of perhaps the smallest of big-league ballplayers, and one of baseball's greatest shortstops, amused and amazed the baseball world for almost three decades!

### A HOUSE OF LAUGHTER

There are many ball parks in America but only one Ebbets Field. Many incredible things have happened there. Right from the beginning, Ebbets Field was tagged as a daffy place, and some of the oddest ballplayers in history called it home.

On the very first day Ebbets Field was to open, not a soul of that huge and eager crowd could gain admission to the park. For it was discovered that the keys to the gates had been lost. It took more than an hour for locksmiths to fit new keys and admit the impatient throng which had gathered to witness the opening-day ceremonies.

Came the parade to the center-field flagpole. In a most impressive array, behind the blaring music of a band, marched Charley Ebbets, the owner of the Brooklyn club, all his players, the mayor of the city, and many celebrities. However, when they reached the flagpole, it was discovered that there was no flag to hoist!

Once, at an opening game, a Brooklyn pitcher struck out the first batter to face him. Then someone remembered that a famous guest had been invited to throw out the first ball. So after one rival batter had already been retired, the game was begun again to permit the guest of honor to throw out the first ball to start the contest.

Years ago, when Babe Herman was Brooklyn's mightiest home-run slugger, a milkman used to hitch his horse and wagon to a post outside Ebbets Field, enter the ball park, and pitch to Herman for daily batting practice.

At Ebbets Field Babe once hit a three-bagger with the bases full, which only resulted in a triple play with all runners winding up on third base!

At Ebbets Field in a world-series game, for the only time in history, Bill Wambsganss of the Cleveland Indians made an unassisted triple-play!

At Ebbets Field a pitcher named Johnny Vander Meer hurled his second consecutive no-hit game, to make baseball history!

The ball park was built in 1913 by a portly exbookkeeper, Charley Ebbets by name. He was something of a character himself. He built this stadium for his sickly boy. He wanted him to have a place to sit in the sun and get plenty of fresh air. Ironically, upon Charley Ebbets' death, his son never gained possession of that ball park. For about twenty years he battled for it in the courts until he finally died, alone and penniless, in a cheap rooming house in the shadow of Ebbets Field.

# BONERS,
## SKULLS, AND GOATS 👉

## ☛ THE BASE HE FORGOT TO TOUCH

September 23, 1908, was a fine day for a ball game. The skies were clear. The sun was shining with friendly warmth. And Fred Merkle was a Giant.

For the Wisconsin-born Merkle, it was great to be alive and a Giant. Fate had brought him to the Polo Grounds and made him one of a group destined to shape baseball history.

The New York Giants were to play mighty Chicago, of "Tinker-to-Evers-to-Chance" fame. The Cubs were champions of the world, now seeking a third consecutive league pennant. However, John McGraw's Giants had more than just hate for the high-riding leaders. They had pennant hopes all their own. This was the day to cash in their dreams of glory and revenge.

Before the game started, Fred Tenney, the Giants' veteran first baseman came to McGraw and complained he was suffering with the miseries of lumbago. So Fred Merkle was assigned to play first. He was to remember that day for the rest of his life.

The game started. It was a brilliant pitching duel between the Giants' immortal Christy Mathewson, and Chicago's Jack Pfeister. The ninth inning found

89

the teams locked in a 1-all score, as the Giants came up to bat.

The capacity crowd jamming every corner of the Polo Grounds became wildly alive as thousands of partisan voices roared for a victory. Devlin lined out a sharp single. The next batter, Moose McCormick hit a grounder, forcing Devlin at second, and barely escaped a double play. Then up to bat came young Fred Merkle. He sent the home-town rooters wild as, with all the confidence of youth, he socked one of Pfeister's best pitches—for a single. Fred Merkle was now perched on first, and his teammate, McCormick, was on third. Kid Bridwell then slammed a clean single to center field. McCormick came prancing happily home with the winning run. The game was over. The Giants had beaten the hated Cubs by a score of 2 to 1, and a pennant looked closer than ever before. Then, something happened. To this day, the mystery of that moment has never been fully solved.

On the winning hit, young Fred Merkle ran halfway to second base. When he saw the winning run score, he promptly turned and ran for the clubhouse to escape the hysterical mob which had flowed on the field. Suddenly, above the din and confusion, Fred Merkle heard a voice scream hysterically. It froze him in his tracks. It was the raspy voice of baseball's famous "little crab," Chicago's second baseman, Johnny Evers. He was yelling to his outfielder teammate, "Circus Solly" Hofman: "The ball! . . . The ball! . . . Get me that ball!"

Outfielder Hofman, aware that the Giants' victory was not complete, threw the ball to Johnny Evers, but it never reached him. By that time, Giant pitcher Joe McGinnity rushed out on the field and intercepted the throw. For a few fleeting seconds, he fought off three frantic Cub players who tried to tear the ball from his grip. But "Iron Man" McGinnity finally heaved it far away into the crowd. Meanwhile, other Giant players seized the dazed Fred Merkle and hustled him back to second, to touch the base. He actually did touch second base long before wily Johnny Evers got hold of another baseball and touched the bag with it. Evers rushed to the umpires, Emslie and O'Day, and demanded that they make a decision on the play. He argued that since Fred Merkle had failed to touch second, it was a force-out; that the winning run did not count, for two men were out. The debate waxed furious, as orators from both teams besieged the confused umpires. Finally, umpire-in-chief Hank O'Day made his decision. He ruled that Fred Merkle was out for his failure to touch second, and that the winning run did not score. Since it was impossible to continue the game, O'Day ruled the game had ended in a tie.

The entire country waited for an official decision by Harry Pulliam, then the President of the National League. Seven days later it came. The game was to be played over. The final day of the scheduled season found the Giants and the Cubs tied for the pennant. The teams had to replay the disputed game.

In the darkness of the dugout was Merkle, "the goat," a heartbroken young man praying with every pitch for a victory. But it was not to be. The New York club lost that play-off game and with it the National League pennant.

Thus Fred Merkle became a marked man for the rest of his life, ever to be remembered as "the bonehead who forgot to touch second," a mistake that had cost his team the flag.

After the game Fred Merkle entered the Giants' clubhouse, his mind made up. He was a pitiful sight.

"It was all my fault," he said. None of his teammates answered him. Then into the room walked John J. McGraw, the toughest loser in baseball and a managerial wizard who never had any use for baseball misfits. Tears streamed down Fred Merkle's face as he turned to McGraw.

"Mr. McGraw," he said, "I'm sorry I lost the pennant for you. I'm quitting baseball forever. I don't belong in the game."

Whereupon tough John McGraw roughly snapped at him: "I'm not firing you, Merkle, and I'm not going to let you quit because of that one boner. Hell, boy, you're a real comer. I'm going to use you for a long time. Don't mind what they'll say about you. They'll make your life miserable, but in spite of them you're going to become a fine first baseman."

Fred Merkle did. For more than twelve years he starred in the major leagues. But to this day all that is remembered of Fred is that he was "the bonehead who forgot to touch second."

However, few there are in baseball who know that on that fateful day, when he forgot to touch second, Fred Merkle was just a rookie playing his first complete game in the majors—a boy only eighteen years old!

### ☞ A SLIP OF THE MIND

One afternoon, Wilbert Robinson became disgusted with the stupidity of his players. So, before game time, he gathered them in a huddle and said that from now on any dumbbell who pulled a "skull" would be fined $10. Then in all his jolly dignity, he waddled up to the umpire-in-chief and handed him a *laundry ticket* instead of the Brooklyn batting order.

### ☞ ANYBODY CAN MAKE A MISTAKE

Bill Klem, in his glory as the greatest of umpires, always boasted that he never "called one wrong." He must have forgotten a certain episode in Pittsburgh.

One afternoon, the Pirates were giving Klem a riding. Finally he lost his patience, strutted over to the Pittsburgh dugout, and roared: "One more word or a wisecrack out of any of you and I'll clear the bench!"

The players fell silent. A Pirate pinch hitter came to bat. He was a rookie up for the first time in the big leagues. The boy was quite jittery when he announced his name to Bill Klem. The ump didn't hear it.

"Speak up, man!" snapped angry Bill Klem, "What's your name?"

And the rookie replied: "Booe!"

Bill Klem's face turned fiery red: "You fresh kid —get off the field—you're out of the game for being too smart!"

Then out of the Pittsburgh dugout the Pirate manager came rushing:

"What's the matter with you, Klem—d'ja go out of your head? This pinch hitter's name is Everett Booe—"B-o-o-e"—and he wasn't trying to kid you!"

That was the only time the great Bill Klem was forced to change his decision and admit he had pulled a boner.

### ☞ NO ANGEL IN THE OUTFIELD

In his youth, Fred Snodgrass played a lot of fine baseball as a big-league outfielder. But one afternoon he dropped an easy fly, and all his glory was wiped away by that one error, an error that became known as the "$100,000 muff."

It was the final game of the 1912 world series between the New York Giants and the Boston Red Sox—three victories for each team. The chips were down as the teams battled through nine innings, tied 1 to 1. In the first half of the tenth, the Giants broke through with a run, and it looked like the end of the rainbow for them with the incomparable Christy Mathewson on the mound.

Came the last half of the tenth. The first Red Sox batter, a pinch hitter, lifted a long lazy fly to center field. Fred Snodgrass was under it. Suddenly a pop bottle landed in front of him as he waited for the catch. It didn't seem to bother the famous ball hawk. But the ball thudded into his glove, went right through his hands, and fell to the ground. It was unbelievable! Fred Snodgrass, one of the best outfielders in the game, had muffed an easy fly. That error blew the championship for the Giants, for the Sox quickly pushed across two runs and won the game.

Fred Snodgrass's error cost his club and teammates $100,000. The headlines screamed his shame to all the world. All sorts of wild stories soon circulated about poor Fred. Some said McGraw lashed him verbally for his blunder. Others hinted his teammates punched him in a clubhouse brawl after that fatal game.

The fickle sports world had found a goat—another hero to tear down. Fred Snodgrass was the victim. Wherever he went and whatever he did, he found himself pointed out as the "Man Who Made the $100,000 Muff"—the man who lost a championship. Even after he left the big-league diamonds, Snodgrass was a marked man, all his baseball glory forgotten.

## ☛ BUTTERFINGERS IN THE INFIELD

Most of the notorious "goats" of the world series have been famous players!

Back in 1925, Roger Peckinpaugh's sensational shortstopping sparked the Washington Senators to a pennant. On the eve of the series between Washington and Pittsburgh, Roger Peckinpaugh reached the heights when he was voted the most valuable player in the American League. Everybody expected him to emerge from that 1925 classic a shining hero. He did establish a new record in that world series— by making eight errors!

## ☛ DADDY OF ALL BASEBALL BONERS

The player to commit the first "classic blunder" in baseball was John Anderson. To this day, old-timers still call boners "a John Anderson."

Around 1900 Anderson was a star. He was a fine first baseman, and for years had the highest fielding average of all American League first sackers. During his big-league career, he played with the New York Yankees, the St. Louis Browns, and the Washington Senators. Everywhere, he was known as "Honest John," one of the respected players of the game.

When John Anderson was with the Senators, a critical game was being played. It was the ninth inning, two men were out, and Washington was a run behind with the bases full. Perched on first was John Anderson, then ace of all base stealers. Washington needed that game to stay in the pennant race. At bat for Washington was its star slugger.

Suddenly, for no apparent reason, John Anderson made a mad dash for second. He tried to steal with the bases filled! That classic blunder, then and there, ended the game with a Washington defeat.

Overnight, John Anderson became the laughing-stock of the baseball world. His name and his shame became something of a household word. Thereafter, a blunder was ridiculed as "a John Anderson." Everything about John Anderson was forgotten except his boner! Where "Honest John" had been a happy ballplayer with laughter in his heart, he turned gloomy, tortured by needling ridicule. Even when he left baseball, the memory of that boner haunted him. To his dying day, John Anderson suffered the stigma of his mistake.

### ☛ NOBODY WANTED TO HEAR HIS ALIBI

When Heinie Zimmerman started the 1917 world series between the White Sox and the Giants, he was known as one of the top third base-men. But he finished that October classic ever to be remembered as a goat. In the deciding game he suddenly found himself in a foot race from third base to home, chasing Eddie Collins, one of the fleetest men in baseball. He literally pursued the winning run right across the plate! The incident will always be known as "Zimmerman's boner." However, the unlucky Heinie was not entirely at fault on that marblehead play, for his catcher and first baseman had left home plate unguarded. But no one ever wanted to listen to Zimmerman's alibi, as with characteristic toughness he summed up his defense: "Who th' h . . . was I going to throw the ball to—the umpire?"

## ☞ ROCK-A-BYE BABY

No ballplayer ever committed a more freakish boner than the once great pitcher, "Fat" Freddy Fitzsimmons. Oddly enough, it happened off the field. One balmy evening, he was rocking himself on a hotel porch, resting before the dining room opened, when he suddenly let out a blood-curdling yell. Fitzsimmons had dozed off and accidentally got the fingers of his famed pitching hand under the rocker and crushed them. It took him a long time to get back into form, and he cost his club many games.

## ☞ ANYWAY HE WAS THERE THAT DAY

The unhappiest of all world-series goats was pitcher Clarence Mitchell. He went into the 1920 classic between the Cleveland Indians and the Brooklyn Dodgers as a well-known big-league hurler. But in the fifth game, the first time pitcher Mitchell came to bat, he hit into a double play. The next time the Brooklyn pitcher took his turn at the plate, two of his teammates were on base. So he lined right to Cleveland's second baseman, Bill Wambsganss, who promptly made the first and only unassisted "triple play" in world-series history. Thus in only two times at bat, pitcher Clarence Mitchell hit into five outs!

## ☞ DOWN WENT THE BOOM

Another world-series boner occurred in 1929, when the Philadelphia Athletics played the Chicago Cubs. As the A's went to bat in the last of the seventh inning of the fourth game, the score was 8 to 0 against them. The Cubs' pitcher, Charlie Root, had allowed but two hits and was trying for a shutout. Up to bat came Al Simmons, the mighty slugger. Instead of pitching safely to him, the confident Charlie Root tried to strike him out. It was a fatal mistake. For Root grooved one and Simmons connected for a home run. The explosion that followed made series history. Before the side could be retired, 15 men came to bat. The Athletics made 10 hits, and 10 runs crossed the plate. It was the most sensational inning in world-series annals. Charlie Root, who should have been a hero, with an 8-to-0 shutout, lost the game 10 to 8 and is remembered as a goat.

## ☞ YOU CAN BE WRONG TWICE

A baseball scout's discoveries can make a pennant team; his costly mistakes can ruin it.

Once there was a big-league scout who made two prize "boots," which is not the record, but this scout made both his mistakes in one day!

Years ago, he arrived in Portsmouth to do business with Frank Lawrence, owner of the Portsmouth club of the Piedmont League.

That afternoon a southpaw was on the mound for the Portsmouth team, and he was doing a whale of a job. The club owner anxiously asked: "Do you want this left-hander? You can have him for a song."

"Naw!" growled the big-league scout, "The kid is too small. He'll never make the big leagues."

Disappointed, the owner of the club directed the scout's attention to the second baseman.

"What about this infielder?" he asked. "Want him?"

The scout watched the player for a few innings, then shook his head again. He grumbled, "Too small."

So, in one afternoon, a big-league scout turned down two obscure players because of their size. He made two of the prize boners of all time. For the pitcher who was too small for the big leagues was Harry Brecheen, who left-handed the St. Louis Cards to a pennant and won three games in the world series. And the second baseman sparked the Brooklyn Dodgers, the Boston Braves, and the New York Giants to pennants. His name—Eddie Stanky.

☞ HIS LAST FLING

In the 1944 series between the St. Louis Cardinals and the St. Louis Browns, the Browns' star shortstop, Vern Stephens, made a bad throw to his second baseman on an easy double-play ball. It paved the way for three Cardinal runs that lost the game and the world-series championship. It proved to be a costly $45,000 error.

### ☞ HE PUT HIS FOOT IN HIS MASK

A catcher's mask once lost a world series. It happened in 1924 when the Giants played Washington for the championship. It was the seventh and final contest. The score was tied in the last inning, with Washington at bat, two were out, and Muddy Ruel was the hitter. With two strikes on him, he lifted a high foul. Hank Gowdy, the Giants' catcher, ripped off his mask and went after the ball to make an easy out. But Hank tripped over his own mask, fell flat on his face, and muffed the ball. Given a new life, Muddy Ruel hit the next pitch for a two-bagger and, a moment later, on a teammate's single, crossed the plate with the winning run.

### ☞ NIGHT MUST FALL

In the 1922 world series, when the Yankees met the Giants, with the game tied at 3 to 3 in the tenth inning, although it was still broad daylight and the sun was shining, play was called "on account of darkness." The club owners had to donate all the gate receipts of the game to charity, to square that colossal "boner" made by the umpires.

## ☛ JUST FOR THE EXERCISE

Even the immortal Babe Ruth once came out of a world series in disgrace. It happened in 1926, in the ninth inning of the seventh and last game, with his team a run behind. The famous Babe tried to steal second in a mad and senseless dash to glory. For at that moment, the rival second baseman had the ball. So the famous Ruth was ludicrously tagged out, and a promising rally was killed, as the Cardinals licked the New York Yankees for the championship.

## ☛ MICKEY'S MISHAP

Anything can happen in baseball—with an assist from a boner. A world series game was actually lost after it had already been won. The diamond magician responsible for this reverse miracle was the once famous catcher, Mickey Owen.

In the fourth game of the 1941 world series between the Brooklyn Dodgers and the New York Yankees, the Brooks led 7 to 4, with two out. Tommy Henrich, the last Yankee slugger at bat, took a third strike to end the game. But the Brooklyn catcher dropped the ball. Before Mickey Owen could recover it, the batter safely reached first.

That boner was all the Yankees needed to come from behind and win the decisive game.

### ☛ SOMEBODY SHOULD HAVE TOLD HIM

Smart ballplayers can look terribly dumb, at times, because of a boner.

In the world series of 1925, the Washington Senators played the Pittsburgh Pirates. Everybody was there, including the President of the United States. They even had four umpires. Yet, no man's hand was raised to save Earl McNeely from committing a boner that was to make him a ludicrous figure. For in one of the games, he sat dreaming while a teammate bilked him out of his turn at bat.

### ☛ PENNY WISE AND POUND FOOLISH

It's a strange gamble—this game of shelling out money for untried rookies. Sometimes a club owner pays a fortune in "bonus bait" and winds up with a lemon. And sometimes an owner turns thrifty, refuses to spend a few dollars for a rookie, and loses a baseball gold mine.

Legend has it that, a long time ago, the Pittsburgh Pirates refused to sign a pitcher because he wanted a bonus of $9. A traveling salesman had spotted that boy on the sand lots of Idaho. He contacted the Pittsburgh manager, a friend of his. But the club owner refused to advance $9—the price of the railroad ticket which would have brought that sand-lot wonder to the city. The rookie pitcher whom Pittsburgh lost for want of the bonus, finally managed to crash the big leagues on his own. He lasted twenty years and became one of the great pitchers of all time—the fabulous "Big Train," Walter Johnson!

Once, the Chicago Cubs refused to part with $25,000 for a prospect with big-league ambitions. The rookie became well known as Marty Marion, an all-round ballplayer who completely dominated his era as a shortstop and batsman.

If that was a blunder, there was another time when this same Chicago club refused a bonus to one untried rookie outfielder. The rookie who was lost for want of a $3,000 inducement became the leading home-run slugger in baseball today—Ralph Kiner!

However, the biggest blunder of them all occurred years ago when a club owner in the Pacific Coast League pleaded with the Cubs to buy a certain player.

"Take him on a trial basis," said the owner. "Keep him for a while and give him a thorough tryout. If you're not satisfied that he can make the grade, the deal is off, and I'll return the purchase price."

But the Chicago club refused that generous offer. And the ballplayer they turned down was Joe DiMaggio!

# A MIXTURE
# OF SOUPBONES

## 🖝 A PRESENT FOR MOTHER

When Bob Feller was just a youngster, his father, a semipro ballplayer, set out to develop Bob into a Hall-of-Fame baseball hero. But it was Bob's mother who encouraged, inspired, and helped him become one of the best.

When Bob was just a small fry whom fate seemed to have designed for the quiet monotony of farm life, it was his mother who encouraged him to play catch in the living room. As Bob grew older, and he and his father moved their baseball lessons to the pastures behind the family barn, there to play far past twilight, it was Ma Feller who always understood and never complained. Instead, she encouraged her son by saying, "You can always eat supper after dark when you can't play baseball."

When neighbors scoffed at Mrs. Feller for permitting her son to waste time playing catch, she would say to them proudly: "Maybe when my boy grows up he'll be a big-league ballplayer. Some day I'll be going to the city to see my Bobby pitch."

That dream came true. At the age of seventeen, Bob Feller signed with the Cleveland Indians.

The shy Iowa farm boy blazed to baseball fame like a flaming meteor. With his "fireball pitch" of incredible speed, he set unbelievable strike-out records. He won more than 200 games as a major-league hurler, and three times pitched no-hit and no-run classics.

However, it was some years after Bob had established himself before his mother came for the first time to see him play in a major-league game, and it was very nearly her last.

It was on Mother's Day in 1939, when Mrs. Feller arrived in Chicago. Bob was to hurl for Cleveland against the White Sox. A happy son met his mother at the train. Proudly, Bob drove her to Comiskey Park and seated her in the private box he had re-

served, close to the playing field. For Ma Feller, it was a rare Mother's Day gift as, for the first time, she saw her famous son walk to the pitcher's mound in a big-league stadium and heard the cheers cascade from the stands.

The game started. It was in one of the early innings that a Chicago batter swung desperately at one of Feller's fast balls and tipped a foul that went sailing into the crowded stands. Fans ducked. The

ball rocketed into the stands near the field boxes, and as fate would have it, out of more than thirty thousand people in that ball park, it struck a gentle lady—Bob's mother. The foul ball knocked her unconscious.

She was rushed to a hospital for emergency treatment. It was a frightened boy who kept vigil at his mother's bedside, fearing the worst. For Bob, the joy of that Mother's Day celebration had turned into a nightmare.

Finally, she awakened. In the privacy of that hospital room it was Ma Feller who comforted her famous son, instead of Bob his mother.

"Don't blame yourself for what happened today, Bobby," she said. "To have been with you on this Mother's Day, and to have seen you pitch, is a happiness I'll never forget. Go on pitching and be the great baseball player they all say you are."

Ma Feller recovered, and Bob went on to become what his mother wanted him to be—one of the finest pitchers of modern baseball.

### ☛ THE DEAD PITCHER WHO WON A GAME

Years ago in a bush-league ball park in Minnesota, a fantastic episode took place. It happened during a game between the teams of Willmar and Benson. At the end of nine innings, it was a scoreless tie. In the first half of the tenth, the Benson club scored a run. Up to bat for the last

half of that inning came the Willmar team. Thielman, the pitcher, cracked out a single. The next
batter lashed one deep into the outfield for what
appeared to be an inside-the-park home run. The
two men on base raced to score. The Willmar pitcher
was a weary ballplayer when he began to leg it
around the sacks on the hit. He just about managed
to stagger into third, and as he rounded the bag, he
collapsed in his tracks. His teammate came pound-
ing toward him. The fallen pitcher lay on the base
line, blocking the way to the plate. Without hesitation, the runner picked up Thielman and actually
carried him across home plate. The umpire allowed
the two runs to count, which gave the Willmar team
a victory. But the Willmar pitcher never knew he
had helped his team win that game, for when he
was carried across with the tying run, he was already
dead of heart failure.


### ☛  A HAYSEED FOR A RIDE

Once, a farmer became a big-leaguer only
because a man needed a hundred dollars. And he
remained in the majors only because a famous ballplayer had made fun of him. Denton Tecumseh
Young, a farmer playing for Canton of the Tri-State
League, was sold to Cleveland for $100 simply be-
cause the club owner needed that amount in a hurry.

Cy Young reported to Cleveland just as the team
was about to play an important series with the Chi-

cago White Stockings, led by the incomparable Cap
Adrian Anson. Cy was a huge man, well over 200
pounds. There wasn't a uniform in the Cleveland
clubhouse that would fit the big rookie. So the manager summoned a tailor, who quickly made him a
suit from left-over material. The uniform fitted
him badly and made him look ridiculous. Thus, gro-
tesquely garbed, Cy Young came out to take the
mound for Cleveland. When the crowd saw the
rookie pitcher, gales of laughter swept the ball park.
The opposing players decided to have some fun with
the odd-looking hayseed. Cap Anson pulled his own
uniform out of shape to imitate Cy Young. He par-
odied Cy's shambling gait. The fans and the players
howled. The big rookie farmer was furious at the
cruelty of a baseball star who was using him as the
butt of his jokes.

"Don't mind Cap Anson, kid," said Cy Young's
manager. "Just pitch carefully to him, so he won't
slug too many homers against you."

But Cy calmly replied: "Cap Anson ain't gettin'
no homers on me today. I'm gonna strike 'im out
every time he comes to bat."

He did. Cy Young won the game, allowing but
three scratch hits.

Immediately afterward, a subdued and impressed
Cap Anson came to owner Frank Robinson and
offered him the stupendous sum of $2,000 in cash
for the rookie pitcher. But the Cleveland owner
refused to part with the hayseed.

Angrily Cap Anson told him, "You're a fool. Grab

the money. This hayseed will never last in baseball and he'll never look as good as he did today."

But Cap Anson was wrong. Cy Young starred for twenty-three years in the big leagues. He compiled the greatest pitching record in history, winning 511 games.

### HE LOST THE LAST BATTLE

It has always been quite a feat for a big-league pitcher to win 20 games in one season. Yet, there was once a pitcher who racked up the astounding total of 41. And he considered that season the unhappiest of the fifteen years he spent in baseball.

In the year 1904, Big Jack Chesbro was the work horse of the old New York Highlanders, predecessors of the present-day Yankees. He was phenomenal. Chesbro seemed unable to pitch a losing game as he passed the 20 mark and successively ticked off 30, 35, and 41 victories.

Then came the last day of that season, and Chesbro went after his forty-second triumph. But in the ninth inning he made one wild pitch which not only lost the game but cost his team the pennant.

Thus, by an ironic and cruel twist of fate, Jack Chesbro is remembered largely for blowing a pennant on the final play of the last game of a baseball season.

### ☛ WYOMING STORY

The story began years ago in the boom town of Lander, Wyoming. That growing, prosperous community was proud of its crackerjack baseball team. Whenever they played another town, the natives of Lander would back their team with cheers, fists, and money.

One day, gloom shrouded the town, for the team's star pitcher had been lured away by a near-by community. Something had to be done.

So a group of the town's leading citizens decided to take action to assure the continued success of the Lander ball club. Some turned baseball scouts as they scoured the West and Middle West in search of a good pitcher.

An alert townsman heard that a young semipro pitcher in Illinois, Lester Hunt, had hurled a no-hit game. He promptly brought him to Lander to pitch for the home team.

Lester Hunt made the natives of Lander mighty proud as he scored victory after victory.

At the end of that season, the people of Lander persuaded him to remain in Wyoming. So pleased were they with this young pitcher from Illinois that they gave him a job, gifted him with a house to live in, and introduced him to the prettiest girl in town. That was the clincher. Lester Hunt fell in love and married her.

It was the beginning of an unusually successful career. As the years passed by, the love and respect which the citizens of Lander had for their star pitcher spread throughout the state. And Lester Hunt, who had been brought to Wyoming because he had pitched a no-hit game for a semipro team in Illinois, became the Governor of Wyoming and in time, was elected to the United States Senate!

👉 **IF HE ONLY FELT BETTER**

The old-timers of the game had novel cures for a sore arm. There was Hoss Radbourne, who was one of the truly great hurlers even though he suffered with a permanently sore arm. When he went

to the mound, his pitching arm ached so that he would begin his warm up by rolling the ball to his catcher. Then someone would rub him with horse liniment. Finally, Old Hoss Radbourne would start throwing. That was the way he pitched for eleven years, and he won 308 games. His record of 60 victories, with 26 in succession, made in the baseball season of 1884, has never been equaled.

☛ **DIZZY AND DAFFY**

There aren't many pitchers around today like Dizzy and Daffy Dean. Dizzy, who hurled less than a half dozen seasons in the majors before his arm went lame, won 133 games.

No sooner did the incredible hick from Arkansas reach the big leagues than he began to boast that he was the greatest pitcher in baseball. He also began to brag about a kid brother back in the hills who was almost as good as himself. So the St. Louis Cards brought up Dizzy's brother, Paul, and Dizzy and Daffy began to turn the majors upside down! Before the 1934 baseball season began, Dizzy bragged that he and Paul would win 45 games. Everybody laughed, but Dizzy and Daffy won 49 and hurled the Cards to a pennant! Before the world series, Dizzy announced that he and his brother would win 4 games. They did—and took the baseball championship of the world for the Cards!

When Dizzy and Daffy pitched, they permitted

no one to tell them what to do. Frankie Frisch was the St. Louis manager at the time. It drove him simply wild. The clowning Dizzy loved to needle him.

One September day in 1934, the Cards were scheduled to play a double-header against the pennant-driving Brooklyn Dodgers. Dizzy was assigned to hurl the first game, Daffy the second.

In the clubhouse, player-manager Frankie Frisch gathered his team to map out the strategy for that day.

As Frisch started reviewing the Brooklyn line-up, explaining to Dizzy how to pitch to each hitter, Dizzy held up his hand:

"Now take it easy, Frankie. I've won twenty-six games so far this season and it don't look exactly right for no infielder like you telling a star like me how to pitch a game o' ball."

Manager Frisch blew his top. He screamed at Dizzy: "All right, you crazy clown—you can pitch any way you want, and get your ears pinned back! I just don't care anymore!"

Dizzy simply grinned and replied, "Aw, now, Frankie, don't get excited. You got nuthin' to worry about with me and Paul around. Them Dodgers will be lucky if they get one hit off'n me or Paul this afternoon."

Dizzy blissfully hiked to the mound and, with effortless motion, won the game. He allowed Brooklyn a single hit! Then Daffy took the hill for the second contest of that afternoon, and also won. He hurled a no-hitter!

The strange twist to the amazing story of Dizzy and Daffy, the greatest brother combination in baseball history, is that when Dizzy finally reached the end of baseball's glory trail, almost on the very same day, his brother Paul lost all his pitching skill and never regained it.

### ☛ HE STOOD ON HIS OWN LEG

Just a few years ago, Bert Shepard was the most talked-about player in the big leagues. One club owner actually tried to kidnap him, while another threatened court action to keep him as a pitcher.

Bert Shepard had returned from World War II, an Air Force hero with a chest full of medals. He became a pitcher for the Washington Senators, although war injuries plagued him so that he underwent five operations on his legs.

He had a brief career as a major-league moundsman. And although his moment of big-league glory was short, he carved his name in the record books. For Bert Shepard was the sole hurler to pitch in the major leagues even though he was a cripple— a man with only one leg.

### ☛ THE FARMER IN THE GILDED CAGE

Do you know who was "the greatest" relief hurler of all time?

He was a bald-headed dirt farmer from Hollis,

Oklahoma. His name was Wilcy Moore. Years ago, he toiled for the New York Yankees. His success tale was a strange one.

Toward the close of the 1926 season, Ed Barrow, boss and builder of the Yankee dynasty, was reading a baseball newspaper. He came across a one-line squib that read:

"W. Moore—pitcher for Greenville—won 30, lost 4."

Barrow made inquiries and was informed that W. Moore was an eccentric farmer who has been pitching in the bushes for years. But he couldn't throw a curve. However, Barrow figured that a hurler who could win 30 games in any league must have something. So he paid $2,500 for him, sight unseen, and Wilcy Moore became a member of the most famous team in the game.

When he arrived at the Yankee camp, the boss had some misgivings about his purchase. Although Moore claimed to be twenty-eight, he looked like a very tired thirty-five. But Wilcy made a big hit right from the start, particularly with Babe Ruth. The Sultan of Swat loved to needle Wilcy about his hitting. Babe called Moore "the worst hitter in the history of baseball," and once bet him $300 to $15 that Wilcy couldn't make five hits all season. Moore got the five, although he garnered his fifth safety on the next to the last day of that baseball season. When Moore returned to his Oklahoma farm, he wrote the Babe a letter in which he reported:

"The $300 I won from you came in handy. I used

it to buy a fine pair of jackasses. I named one 'Babe' and the other 'Ruth.' . . ."

In his first year in the majors, Wilcy Moore proved to be the finest relief pitcher of record. He was in 50 games for the Yankees! He won 19 on his own, and saved many others for his faltering mates. Moore finished with the best earned-run average in the league. He not only helped the Yankees to win the flag, but when they reached the world series, which they were to take in four straight games, it was Wilcy Moore who relieved successfully in the first game, and won the windup.

Such is the odd story of the great relief pitcher. But perhaps the strangest part of this tale is that, at the time Moore was hailed as the greatest relief pitcher in big-league history, the Yankees paid him the munificent sum of $1,800 for the season!

Times sure have changed!

### ☞  THE RELUCTANT HERO

One afternoon back in the season of 1920, Walter Johnson came to the ball park and, for the first and only time in his career, complained of a sore arm. It was so lame that he had to use his left hand to brush his teeth. But since he was Washington's biggest attraction, and the Senators were to play an important game against the Boston Red Sox, Clark Griffith sent Johnson to the mound.

"Try for just one inning," said Griffith, "and if your arm gives you trouble I'll take you out."

Johnson, sore arm and all, got by the first frame without the Red Sox scoring. He wanted to quit, but the big boss coaxed him to try just one more. So it went, until Johnson, wincing with pain at every pitch, twirled his way through nine innings.

Strangely enough, on the *only* day Walter Johnson ever showed up in a ball park with a sore arm, he pitched the *only* no-hit game of his twenty-year career in the majors, the only no-hitter in the 413 victories he chalked up as the immortal "Big Train."

## TWO STINGY PITCHERS

In the season of 1917, Fred Toney pitched for Cincinnati, and Big Jim Vaughn was a star hurler for the Chicago Cubs. Toney and Vaughn were bitter rivals.

One day the two happened to meet away from the ball park, and they began to kid each other about their abilities. The joshing got out of hand, and finally Jim Vaughn snapped at Toney: "Listen, you bum, the next time I pitch against you, I'll let that tramp team of yours down with no hits!"

Fred Toney, a big, easygoing, likable guy, laughed in derision and retorted, "Jim, when you do, I'll always go you one inning better!"

For quite a while thereafter, both pitchers waited for the day when the schedule would pit them against one another. That day came on the afternoon of May 2nd.

Both Toney and Vaughn were in superb form; inning after inning, neither pitcher allowed a single hit.

It was a duel that had the fans on the edge of their seats. To see one pitcher on the way to a no-hitter is rare indeed. But to see two doing the trick was something that could only happen in storybooks. Then came the ninth inning. Two pitchers had performed the impossible. Each had a no-hit, no-run game for the regulation nine innings of play.

However, in the first half of the tenth, Jim Vaughn faltered. Cincinnati scored a run on a single and an error. But in the last half of the tenth, Fred Toney did not allow a hit, and he won the game with a no-hit shutout!

## COURAGE IS WHERE YOU FIND IT

Once Lou Brissie was given up for dead, but he returned to pitch in the majors.

He was a paratrooper corporal during World War II, when his squad was pinned down by artillery fire. A direct hit killed all the men around him. Miraculously, he escaped death. But he was badly wounded, with both legs smashed and shrapnel wounds in hands and shoulders. For hours, Brissie lay in an open field. When the action was over, first-aid men passed him up as dead. He was too weak to call for help, but fortunately a medic noticed him move slightly. His life was saved, and Brissie returned home—on crutches.

And although Lou Brissie suffered the anguish of twenty-three operations, to live, walk again, and play baseball, he became one of the best pitchers in the major leagues.

### ☛ HE WAS NO DUMMY

Around 1900, Luther Taylor played for the New York Giants. Although his pitchingmates were such immortals as Christy Mathewson, Snake Ames, and "Iron Man" Joe McGinnity, Luther Taylor was a star in his own right. For he was not only a winner, but one of the most colorful players of his time. He was a most unique athlete—he was a deaf-mute.

Not so many years ago, the once-famous "Dummy" Taylor found an unknown ballplayer named Dick Sipek, whom he taught and coached into a major-league job as outfielder with the Cincinnati Reds. Oddly enough, "Dummy" Taylor's big-league find was also a deaf-mute.

### ☛ AN EYE FOR FAME

In 1939 Tom Sunkel was on the mound staff of the St. Louis Cardinals. For a while he was also with the New York Giants, and then he returned to the minor leagues. Pitching for St. Paul in the "little world series," Tom Sunkel chalked up a no-hit no-run game against the Louisville Colonels. It was the first no-hitter in play-off history of the American Association. All in all, Tom Sunkel pitched for about fifteen years in organized baseball, even though he was a hurler who was blind in one eye.

### DADDY OF THE CURVE BALL

Pitchers are proud. They're jealous of both reputation and skill. Deny one his rightful claim to fame, and you have a brokenhearted man. One such pitcher was Freddy Goldsmith.

To the modern generation of fans, Freddy Goldsmith may be just a line of type in a dog-eared record book, but there is a pathetic story behind that name. Freddy Goldsmith was "the daddy of the curve ball," and his tragedy was that he fretted himself to death because his right to this glory was disputed.

One day in 1867, in a game with Harvard, Freddy Goldsmith made a great discovery. He learned he could throw a baseball so it would curve. The skeptics laughed at him, so, before a large crowd, he gave a demonstration. A line was drawn along the ground. Poles were set at each end of the line, which was 45 feet long. Another pole was placed midway between those two. Freddy Goldsmith took his place at one pole, and his catcher stood at the other. Then he threw a baseball so that it went on the outside of the center pole and the inside of the others—in a perfect curve. It created a sensation, and Goldsmith became famous as the inventor of the "curve ball."

He was signed to pitch for Cap Anson's Chicago White Stockings, and he won fame as a big-league hurler.

When his baseball days were over, Freddy Goldsmith left the game, confident of his claim to immortality. For years he lived with his memories, a happy man. But one day an official motion picture was issued, telling the story of a hundred years of baseball history. In that motion-picture record, Goldsmith was ignored, and credit for the invention of the curve ball was given to a pitcher named Arthur Cummings. That slight broke up old Freddy Goldsmith. Ill at the time, he sorrowed himself into complete invalidism. He talked of nothing but this injustice. His disappointment was so bitter that he wept constantly. He died clutching a yellowed newspaper clipping which confirmed the most important moment of his entire career—the invention of the curve—a pitch that revolutionized the game.

### ☛ HALF-ARMED FOR GLORY

There have been all kinds of ballplayers searching for fame and fortune in the big leagues, like Hugh Dailey, for instance.

It was some years before the turn of the century when Dailey showed up in the Cleveland camp looking for a job as a pitcher.

The manager shook his head: "Go home and forget it!" he brusquely told the boy. "You don't look like a ballplayer to me."

Hugh Dailey hung around and continued to pester the manager until finally he was given a tryout. He made the batters look ridiculous. Few could hit his fast ball. The surprised manager signed him up for Cleveland. He became a sensation—the most talked-about hurler in the game! One afternoon he set a record as he struck out 19 men in one contest. On another afternoon, Hugh Dailey hurled a no-hit game against Philadelphia.

Dailey pitched for many years, and when his big-league days were over, he still continued to play in the minors until he was fifty-six years old.

Hugh Dailey, one of the greatest pitchers in baseball, was a hurler with only one arm!


### THE LOST FOUR TOES

For more than twenty years Charles "Red" Ruffing was a standout pitcher. During his career he won 270 games, and scored 7 world-series victories, more than any other pitcher.

Ruffing started in baseball as an outfielder and became a pitcher only because of an accident. As a youngster, because of poverty he was forced to work in a coal mine. One day in a mine-pit accident, his left foot was crushed, and four of his toes had to be amputated. That accident changed Red's baseball destiny, for, unable to run fast enough for a semipro outfielder, he became a pitcher—one of the greatest of all time.

### A MOTION PICTURE THAT WAS REAL

For a few years, back in the '30's, Monty Stratton pitched winning ball for the Chicago White Sox. One day, while hunting, he accidentally shot himself. When he came out of the hospital, Stratton was minus a leg. His big-league career was over, although he refused to believe it. For a few years he remained with the Sox trying to come back as a pitcher, but his efforts were pathetic. They made him a coach for the Chicago team, but Monty wanted to play baseball. So he went back to the minors and there he pitched and won a good number of games. The courage of Monty Stratton, the one-legged pitcher, made such an inspiring baseball story that Hollywood immortalized it in a film seen by millions of people the world over.

### THREE FINGERS TO FAME

Around 1900, a youngster working in an Indiana coal mine was trapped in an accident. When he was hoisted to the surface, moaning with pain, he was taken to a hospital with a crushed right hand. That boy recovered, but he lost two fingers. It was a heartbreaking misfortune, because he was a fair pitcher for an amateur baseball team.

He tried to pitch again. One day, while tossing the ball around with a friend, he made a startling discovery. Every time he threw the ball, it slipped off the stubs of his crippled fingers and took a sharp hop. That convinced him. He went to the manager of the Terre Haute team in the old Central League and asked for a job. He was given a tryout, and before long he was pitching for the Chicago Cubs.

Despite his handicap, that three-fingered pitcher became one of the more sensational hurlers during the "Tinker-to-Evers-to-Chance" era. He pitched the Chicago Cubs to 3 National League pennants and 2 world series championships. In the fourteen years he starred in the big leagues, he won 239 games.

History will always remember this pitcher with the handicap as the famed Mordecai "Three-fingered" Brown.


☛    "IRON MAN" JOE

As long as legends of baseball are told, just so long will "Iron Man" Joe McGinnity be remembered as a rugged pitcher of unusual stamina.

The saga of Joe McGinnity is the curious story of a baseball failure who schemed his way to immortality.

A saloonkeeper in Springfield, Illinois, McGinnity yearned to become a famous pitcher. He found himself a job in the minor leagues, but he quickly proved himself—a failure. He was so useless that after only two years in the minors he quit in disgust.

Then one day, while tending bar, Joe conceived an exciting scheme. All the famous hurlers of that day had great speed. Now, what baseball needed was a new delivery—a slow-ball pitcher to bewitch and bewilder the batters. McGinnity planned to be that pitcher with the new delivery.

He mapped his campaign for big-league fame and fortune. Slowly but surely, he developed an underhand delivery, and before long he had left his saloon for a berth in the big leagues.

With his soft pitches and amazing control, McGinnity became the most durable pitcher in the game. For the legendary Baltimore Orioles, he won 5 games in 6 days. Another time, he won 11 games in 12 days! He won a pennant for Brooklyn with 30 victories; and he won another pennant for the Giants with 35. He became famous and feared as the "Iron Man" of baseball. In one month alone, the "Iron Man" pitched and won 3 double-headers.

After eleven brilliant years in the major leagues, McGinnity began to coast downhill. Finally, he wound up in the minors, but he pitched in professional baseball until he was fifty-two years old!

## 🖝 HIT THE ROAD

Late in the summer of 1917, Eddie Plank
was in a St. Louis uniform pitching against Walter
Johnson. On that August afternoon, Plank was mag-
nificent! He hurled the finest game he had ever
pitched in all his seventeen years as a major-league
hurler, with 320 wins. He allowed only 2 scratch
hits, doubtful blows that well could have been scored
as errors. But instead of winning, he lost that game
1 to 0. He lost because of the sloppy support he
received from his mediocre teammates.

So Eddie Plank, fierce in his pride as a pitcher,
became so disgusted that he stuffed his glove in his
pocket, walked off the field without saying a word
to anyone, quickly dressed, and, without even a
good-bye, left the St. Louis ball park never to return
again or to pitch in another big-league game!

## 🖝 A SWITCH IN TIME

In baseball lore are a handful of success
stories of ballplayers on the brink of obscurity who
became famous stars.

There was an infielder, for example. After a long
and dreary spell as a mediocre third baseman for the
Philadelphia Phillies, he switched, to become a
pitcher good enough to win almost 200 games. His
name was Bucky Walters.

But the most phenomenal transformation is that of Bob Lemon, who also sought fame as a third sacker.

Lemon was a third baseman for the Cleveland Indians, and he was a flop! So he became an outfielder for Cleveland, and he was also a flop. He was so poor that, in the season of 1947, he said to his manager, conscious-stricken and discouraged: "I'm no good to you, to the team, or to myself. Send me away!"

Strictly from desperation, Bob Lemon switched to hurling. Almost overnight he converted himself into one of baseball's most valuable pitchers, to become one of the best-known stars in the sports world.

☛ HE STARTED THE 20 CLUB

How many of the faithful know who was the first pitcher to win 20 games in one season? It is the story of an unknown who became a great pitcher—because of homesickness!

Away back in the '60's, a seventeen-year-old farm boy named Albert Goodwill Spalding came to Rockford, Illinois, to live with a relative. Homesick in a strange town, that unhappy boy sought solace for his loneliness.

At the time, Rockford was the home of the great Forest City baseball team. One afternoon, while Albert Spalding reclined on a grassy bank watching the Forest City nine practicing, a ball bounded his way. He picked it up and returned it to one of the players with such speed and accuracy that the owner promptly made him an offer to pitch. Lonely, home-sick Albert Spalding accepted, and embarked on a journey from city to town to play for that famed team. Soon, he was acclaimed the greatest pitcher in the country!

From Rockford, Spalding joined Boston, where he made hurling history. The first year at Boston, he pitched all the games played by that team that year—and won 39. The next year, he pitched in all the 71 Boston games and he won 52! The following season he won 56 games, of which 24 were consecu-tive victories! In his last year for Boston, he won 47 games. When Albert Spalding, who had become Bos-ton's most famous sports hero, decided to pitch for Chicago, enraged citizens rioted, while others tear-fully pleaded with the pitcher not to desert their city.

All in all, Albert Spalding won 252 games as a big-league pitcher. When his active playing days were over, he became a manager, a club owner, a baseball league official, an author of books on baseball, a real-estate operator, a sporting-goods manufacturer, and a millionaire!

In a little park near Baseball's Hall of Fame at Cooperstown, there stands a statue of Albert Good-will Spalding who popularized the game of baseball throughout the world. His name still appears on many of the baseballs used in major-league games.

## COMPLEX PLOTTING
## —STRATEGY AT WORK

The most inspired victory drive in modern baseball was made by the New York Giants of 1951. Starting that season with 11 straight losses, the team found itself, late that year, 16 games away from first place. After a storybook finish, they wound up with the National League pennant.

But the Giants of 1916 actually had a more remarkable winning streak. On one road trip they won 17 straight games. The Giants returned home, lost a few, and then proceeded to weave the most astounding skein of victories. That team won 26 straight games—a record that still stands! Thus, in the space of but a single season, the 1916 Giants built one winning streak of 17 straight, and another of 26. But, strangely enough, that season the team wound up in fourth place!

The longest winning streak in all baseball history belongs to the Cincinnati Red Stockings of old. In 1870 the Cincinnati club came to Brooklyn to play a game against the Atlantics. The Red Stockings were riding the crest of fame, having won 92 straight games.

In the ninth inning the teams were locked in a tie. The excitement was high, for a lot of money had been wagered. At the end of the ninth, with the score still tied and darkness fast approaching, the Brooklyn club wanted to call the game. But Cincinnati was reluctant to leave the field without adding another victory to its amazing total. So the game continued. In the eleventh, Cincinnati scored twice, but in its half of that inning the Atlantics managed to put two men on base. The next batter drove a long fly, and as the Cincinnati outfielder set himself to make the catch, a mob of hoodlums poured out of the stands swinging clubs and flashing knives. The frightened outfielder ran away instead of fielding the ball. As a result, all Brooklyn runners scored, and Cincinnati lost that game 8 to 7. Thus, ended the longest winning streak in baseball history.

## ☞ WHO'S ON FIRST?

Maybe "dusting off" is part of the game, but let it not be forgotten that some great players have been ruined by bean balls.

Fred Clarke, the famous Pittsburgh outfielder and "original" boy manager of the nineteenth century, had an effective way of retaliating for bean balls. Whenever pitchers threw at him, Fred Clarke always bunted and tried to spike the man covering the bag. But innocent ballplayers became victims of that cruel strategem. As a result, a bitter feud developed between Fred Clarke and Boston's famous old first baseman, Fred Tenney. Tenney was spiked by Clarke several times until he himself finally took advantage of the "bean ball" to end that feud.

One afternoon, Tenney fielded a grounder Fred Clarke had hit, but he waited until Clarke got past first. Then, he threw the ball as hard as he could, and he hit Fred Clarke squarely on the head. It knocked Clarke unconscious.

After several minutes, Fred Clarke came out of the fog, wobbled unsteadily to his feet, went over to the first baseman Fred Tenney and said, "Okay, Fred, you win! I'll never try to spike you again just because I'm sore at a pitcher trying to bean me. You win!"

And that was the end of one bitter feud.

### ☞ HEY, "POOSH-'EM-UP" TONY— WHAT DO YOU DO?

When he was pitching for the pennant-winning Yankees, Lefty Gomez was also one of baseball's most celebrated screw balls.

The Yankees were playing an important game, and Gomez was on the mound. His teammate, Tony Lazzeri, was in the midst of a sensational fielding streak, and the papers were making a fuss about the great "Poosh-'em-up" second baseman, calling him a genius of the infield.

In a tight spot during the game, an enemy batter slammed the ball straight at pitcher Gomez, who stopped it, whirled, and for no apparent reason, threw the ball to Tony at second.

When the startled Lazzeri demanded to know what had gotten into Goofy Gomez, the pitcher said solemnly, "I didn't know what to do with that ball, but I've been reading all week that you're the smartest fielder in the world—so I thought I'd give it to you and let you decide!"

### 👉 BLACKBOARD VICTORIES

Years ago, when Branch Rickey was boss of the St. Louis Cardinals, he insisted that his manager, Rogers Hornsby, hold daily blackboard sessions for the team. Strategy was discussed, and plays and situations were planned, while boss Rickey would beam with pleasure.

However, the team continued to lose. One day Rickey saw a flock of reporters trap the gloomy Rajah and ask him how things were working out, to which manager Hornsby replied with a deep sigh: "Fifty-fifty. We play two games every day and always win the morning game on the blackboard."

Branch Rickey held no more blackboard talks.

### 👉 TO WHOM IT MAY CONCERN

Not so many years ago, a youngster, anxious for a career in baseball, caught on as a pitcher with a bush-league team.

From the moment he reported for work, he yearned to burn up that small-time loop. But the manager was reluctant to use him as a hurler. Game after game passed, and the young pitcher remained on the bench, waiting for that big moment when he would receive a starting assignment.

Finally the manager ordered that boy to go to the mound. He began to pitch. His happiness soon changed to misery, for the rival batters found his stuff to their liking. Practically every ball he served up went sailing over the fence for a home run.

After the game the disgusted manager called the pitcher to his side and brusquely broke the bad news to him: "Young feller, I'm afraid you'll never do. I'm going to let you go!"

The kid's eyes popped with surprise as he said, "You mean you're going to release me after I pitched for you only once?"

"That's just what I'm going to do!" snapped the impatient manager.

Anxiously, the young pitcher asked: "At least you'll give me a recommendation, won't you?"

"Oh sure," replied the manager, anxious to be rid of the ambitious kid, and, without further ado, he dashed off a note of recommendation which read:

"To Whom It May Concern: The bearer of this note pitched one game for me and I am satisfied."

With time, that rookie pitcher did much better. He became one of the great players in the major leagues, and one of the most feared batters in the game. His name—Stan Musial.

## ☛ THREE LETTERS TO A CLUB OWNER

When Al Schacht was an obscure busher, he began to angle for a job in the major leagues. He became his own baseball scout, sending daily anonymous letters to Clark Griffith, owner of the Senators. All his notes praised an unknown pitcher named Al Schacht. One letter would inform Clark Griffith that this phenomenal Schacht had struck out 12 men in a game. Another letter told how Schacht had compiled an 8-game winning streak. A third claimed the unknown Schacht was a better pitcher than Walter Johnson. Curiosity finally got the better of Griffith. He gave Al a tryout with Washington and Schacht proved to be one of the worst pitchers in major-league history but one of baseball's most lovable characters (and clowns).

## ☛ BIRTH OF THE BUNT

Not much attention has been paid the originator of the bunt, yet its role in baseball has been important. To a ballplayer named Tim Murnane goes the honor.

Murnane, originally with the Philadelphia Athletics, joined Boston when the National League was formed. Tim was an infielder, and a good one, too. He was a hare on the bases, but at bat he was a bust.

One afternoon he went to the plate for his turn at bat, worried because the manager had soured on him for his weak stickwork. Tim feared that his days as a big-leaguer were numbered.

The enemy pitcher wound up and let go. Tim Murnane saw the ball come sailing plateward; he swung, and by sheer accident, he gave the ball a feeble tap with his bat. The ball stopped dead in front of the pitcher's box. However, Tim Murnane was probably the fastest man of his day, so, before the enemy pitcher could field that ball, speedy Tim reached first base.

That surprising hit set Murnane to thinking. The ballplayer saw an opportunity to regain his manager's favor and win some measure of respect as a batter. He went home, whittled one side of his bat flat, and, in secret, began to practice his new stroke. He became so skilled that he could lay down a bunt in whatever direction he chose.

Thus the "bunt" came to baseball, and Murnane became one of the more dangerous batters in the game. Pitchers began to fear him because he not only upset them but got on base so often that he blew games wide open.

There probably never lived a greater master of the bunt than Tim Murnane, its inventor.

### ☞ BEWARE OF A MAD BALLPLAYER

The Yankees and the Tigers were engaged in a close game. In a late inning, up to bat for the Tigers came silent Charley Gehringer, the greatest second baseman of his day. Several rookies on the New York bench began to shout taunts at the brilliant Gehringer, hoping to rattle him.

They were quickly silenced by the laconic manager, Joe McCarthy, who growled: "Shut up and leave him alone. He's hitting three-forty as it is. Get him mad and he's liable to hit five hundred!"

### ☞ QUIET PLEASE—BALLPLAYER ASLEEP

One afternoon years ago, when Brooklyn was managed by Wilbert Robinson, the Dodgers staged an exciting rally in a game that was seemingly lost. They filled the bases. Up to bat came one of Brooklyn's hard hitters who represented the winning run. Chic Fewster, sitting in the Brooklyn dugout next to manager Robinson, grabbed a bat and began to pound away with it on the dugout steps, as he screamed taunts at the rival pitcher.

"Cut that out!" ordered manager Robinson.

"Why?" asked the surprised Brooklyn player. "Can't I whoop it up to keep the rally going?"

Manager Robinson pointed to a far corner of the

dugout where Brooklyn's star pitcher, Jess Petty, was fast asleep.

"Cut out the noise," ordered the manager. "I don't want you to wake up old Jess."

### ☞ DON'T BLOW YOUR NOSE

Sometimes a clever manager's signals can make him feel like an idiot. When one big-league manager blew his nose, for example, he actually blew away a ball game!

The Cleveland Indians took the field, one afternoon, with Lou Boudreau, their manager, suffering from a bad cold. In a late inning the Indians had runners on first and second, and it looked as if one hit would break up the game. The team's best slugger came to bat. But before he could swing at the first pitch, the two Cleveland base runners started a double steal. One was thrown out at third and the other tossed out at second. The game was over. Manager Boudreau was furious.

"Who signaled a double steal?" he roared at his players.

"You did!" replied one of the culprits. "You took your handkerchief out of your pocket and blew your nose."

"What of it?" screamed the manager.

"Blowing your nose was the sign for the steal. Don't you remember your signals, boss?"

Sure enough, that was the proper sign. The manager had completely forgotten it in the misery of his cold.

### ☛ HE SHOULD HAVE STOOD IN THE DUGOUT

It happened in the season of 1936 when rowdy Dick Bartell was an infielder with the New York Giants. He went into the final game with a batting average of .299.

Before the start of the contest the Giants' manager informed Bartell that if he got a hit early, he would take him out so he could wind up with a .300 batting average. If he finished the season with .300, he was to receive an extra bonus of $1,000 from the club and an increase in pay.

Dick Bartell came to bat for the first time, and he flied out. The second time he grounded out. The third time, he was desperate for a hit.

Cy Pfirman was umpiring at home plate. The first pitch to Bartell he called a strike. Rowdy Dick kept his temper in check, but he gave the umpire a dirty look. The next pitch the umpire called "strike two." Dick Bartell told off Pfirman, with gestures. Cy Pfirman was no Caspar Milquetoast. He "blew his top" and told the player a few things himself. Bartell lit into the umpire full blast. In a moment, he was kicked out of the game. Bartell was boiling, and he challenged the umpire to a fist fight under the stands. The manager and several of his teammates had to hold him. The upshot of the battle was that Dick Bartell ended the season with a batting average of only .298 and lost the bonus. To top it all, he was fined $50 for arguing with an umpire.

The battle cost him a $1,050, a .300 batting average, and a raise in pay!

## ☞ WHO SAID HE WAS A DUMBBELL?

There was no manager quite like the Falstaffian leader of the Brooklyn team during the seventeen years he bossed the Dodgers.

In one tight game, manager Wilbert Robinson ordered his star slugger, Babe Herman, to bunt. The eccentric, happy-go-lucky Babe ignored the sign and connected for a home run. On his return to the dugout, Wilbert Robinson happily greeted his outfielder.

"Atta boy, Babe!" he cried. "That's the way to hit 'em, no matter what any dumbbell tells you!"

## ☞ THE IMPATIENT BABE

John McGraw was the toughest loser in baseball, and he would try anything, however fantastic, to win a game.

During the 1923 world series between the Giants and the Yankees, the Giants had one game sewed up in the early innings. However, in the eighth, with the bases full and two out, up to bat came the dreaded home-run king, Babe Ruth.

Rosy Ryan, pitching for the Giants, somehow managed to slip two strikes past the Babe's thundering bat. Suddenly, McGraw noticed something about Ruth unseen by anyone else in the jammed ball park. He signaled to the Giants' catcher.

Pancho Snyder walked out to the mound and whispered to Ryan: "Mac says to throw the next one into the dirt."

Pitcher Ryan stared at his catcher as he stammered, "Has the Old Man gone crazy?"

"Throw your next pitch at his feet," snapped Snyder. "McGraw says Ruth's so anxious that he'll swing at anything no matter where you put it."

So Ryan fired the ball at Ruth's feet, and sure enough the Babe swung and struck out. A bit of strategy had won another battle.

## ☛ KELLY NOW CATCHING FOR BOSTON

There was one ballplayer who did so many things first and did them so differently that he practically wrote the rules. He was the legendary King Kelly who made "Slide, Kelly, S-L-I-D-E!" a byword of the game.

Often on an infield tap, while the one umpire officiating the game had to watch the play at first, King Kelly would short-cut second base by 20 feet in going from first to third. Similarly, he would cut third in scoring from second. Because of Kelly and his tricky base running, it was found necessary to have more than one umpire to a game.

He was probably the quickest-thinking player of his time. New rules had to be made to keep him from snatching games. One afternoon in 1889, Charley Ganzel was catching for Boston, while King Kelly, the captain of the team, was sitting on the bench. In a late inning, with men on bases, a rival batter hit a towering fly which drifted foul between home and third. The Boston catcher tried to get that high twisting fly, but it was evident that he would never reach it in time. King Kelly leaped from the bench, rushed out on the field, and shouted: "Kelly now catching for Boston!" With nonchalance, he caught the fly and retired the side, squelching a rally that might have won the game. After that, the rule makers wrote a new law which permitted no change of line-up in the course of a game unless announced by the umpire.

## ☞ BALLPLAYERS CAN ALSO CRY

In Detroit, in 1939, Lou Gehrig, captain of the Yankees, walked up to the umpire-in-chief and handed him the New York club's batting order. The ump looked at it casually, then suddenly his mouth popped open with surprise, for he saw Babe Dahlgren's name had been filled in to play first base.

The astounded arbiter said to Gehrig: "What's up, Lou? Isn't there some mistake on this list? Aren't you playing first base as usual?"

Then he quickly stopped asking questions, and turned away with a lump in his throat. For there stood big Lou Gehrig with tears streaming from his eyes. Because, for the first time in fifteen years, he had removed himself from a Yankees' batting order —for the good of the team! His day as a big-league player was over.

When Lou Gehrig, already in the shadow of death, took himself out of the Yankees' line-up after playing in his record-making streak of 2,130 consecutive games, the tension in the New York dugout was terrific. It looked as if none of his teammates would be able to play. But Lefty Gomez, a pal and admirer of Gehrig, broke the spell and saved the situation with a timely wisecrack. For as Gehrig came into the silent dugout, Lefty quipped: "You got no squawk, Lou. It took 'em fifteen years to get you out of the game. It usually takes only a few innings to get me out!"

Everybody laughed, and things were easier that day.

## ☞ TRIPLE PLAY TO FAME

Neal Ball holds a unique place in baseball history because, in a few breathtaking seconds, he leaped from obscurity to fame.

It happened in 1909 when he was playing his first season with the Cleveland Indians. He was a shortstop. Cleveland was meeting the Boston Red Sox.

It was the second inning, and the Sox were at bat with men on first and second and none out. A screaming line drive was hit, and Neal Ball leaped high and grabbed it. He touched second, retiring a runner for the second out, then he ran down the other base runner between first and second, to put out the side!

It was the first unassisted triple play in major-league history!

### ☛ THREE FOR ONE

There was another ballplayer who also made a triple play, but the record books have not listed his claim. It was the most amusing triple killing ever made.

It happened years ago when Larry McLean was a major-league catcher. McLean was also a fast-stepping playboy. One afternoon, he showed up for a game looking quite woozy after a night of merry-making. After a few innings of crouching behind the plate under the hot sun, McLean was in a daze and playing purely by instinct. In a late inning, Larry let a pitch dribble out of his mitt. Hastily throwing off his mask, he pounced on the ball and whirled just in time to see an enemy runner trying to steal home. McLean arrived at home plate at the same time as the umpire and pitcher who had raced in from the mound to take a throw. With everything in a haze, McLean saw three men closing in on the dish. The big catcher, with the ball gripped in his huge fist, tagged the runner, the umpire, and his own pitcher.

"I don't know who in hell the runner is," he shouted, "but I made a triple play, and one of you guys is out!"

### ☞ ALEX SETTLED IT

One morning while Joe McCarthy was manager of the Chicago Cubs, he called a meeting of his team to discuss some strategy to be employed against the Pittsburgh Pirates. The teams were scheduled to play that afternoon. The center of discussion was a former Cub player who had been traded to Pittsburgh. Everyone showed up on time except Chicago's famous pitcher, Grover Cleveland Alexander, who was slated to pitch the game. Finally he came in, looking weary and a bit seedy. Manager McCarthy ignored his entrance as he continued outlining the plans for the game. Alexander flopped into a seat and promptly began to snooze.

"We'll change our signs whenever that player gets on second," instructed McCarthy.

At that point Alex woke up and drawled, "What's all the worryin' about anyway. How's he ever goin' to get on second with me pitching? Besides, Mac, if there was any chance of that guy ever reaching second, you wouldn't have traded him, would you, Mac?"

That ended the strategy meeting.

### ☛ HE SIGNED FOR A STEAK

You may not believe it, but a steak once helped a shrewd manager bring a stubborn holdout to terms.

It happened years ago in spring training. At the time, the New York Giants owned a great pitcher named Jack Scott. He was a thrifty farmer from North Carolina, possessor of an enormous appetite. "Deacon," Scott, as he was known, was one of the best trenchermen in baseball.

That particular spring, Scott showed up at the Giants' training camp—unsigned. He was holding out for more money. McGraw refused to permit the holdout to partake of his daily meals with the rest of the players—at the club's expense. But for several days, Scott stubbornly refused to sign his contract, while his supply of cash dwindled. Soon he was subsisting mostly on sandwiches. The foxy McGraw, knowing that a steak was Scott's weakness, had huge thick steaks served to his players daily. Poor Scott almost went crazy as he watched his teammates gorging themselves. Finally, he could stand it no longer. When dinnertime came, the lean and hungry holdout stormed into the hotel dining room, rushed up to McGraw's table where the manager sat contemplating a steak, and pleaded with him.

"Please, Mr. McGraw," he said, "I'm hungry. Just

let me sit here and eat a steak like that, and I'll sign the darn contract at any figure you say."

"Sit down," ordered McGraw, as he quickly pulled out the contract and a fountain pen. Only after Jack Scott had signed and ended his holdout siege did McGraw smilingly order the waiter to bring a couple of steaks for his star pitcher.

### 👉 THE SMARTER THEY ARE

In the 1934 world series, it was a famous manager who joined the herd of Capricornus. He was Frankie Frisch, pilot of the St. Louis Cardinals, who sent in the great Dizzy Dean, as a pinch runner. Immediately after, on a double play, Dean was hit with the ball on the back of the head, and knocked cold. He was rushed to the hospital while everyone castigated Frisch for risking an injury to his great pitcher in the unnecessary role of a pinch runner.

### 👉 A SUCKER IS BORN EVERY MINUTE

Philadelphia was scheduled to play the St. Louis Browns. The Browns' pitcher, learning that Waddell was to work against him the following afternoon, tricked Rube into an argument over who could throw a baseball farther. Waddell took the bait. The two pitchers met secretly in the ball park early the next morning. The Brown pitcher stood at the fence in center field and faked a throw to home plate.

Rube Waddell sneered and said, "If that's the best you can do, give the ball to a man who can really peg it!"

From the center-field fence, he made as perfect a throw to home as one would want to see.

The St. Louis pitcher pretended amazement. "I bet you can't do it again!"

So Waddell tossed another strike. And again he was challenged, and again he did it.

For almost two solid hours, Rube stood in center field, firing bullets into home plate. The foxy St. Louis pitcher finally admitted that Rube had the stronger arm and handed over the five-dollar bet. He left the ball park chuckling to himself, confident Rube would have nothing left for the game. But that afternoon, Waddell took the mound fresh as a daisy and beat the St. Louis Browns, fanning 14 men for a shutout.

As Rube Waddell was walking off the field, he caught up with the dejected St. Louis pitcher and said, "That was swell practice you gave me this morning."

### ☞ A GOOD ENOUGH REASON

It happened some years ago when fiery Leo Durocher was the manager of Brooklyn.

The Dodgers were playing the Cubs, and there was bad blood between the teams. Brooklyn's pitcher, Whit Wyatt, had beaned a Chicago batter, so Hi Bithorn winged the Dodgers' pride and joy, Dolf Camilli. Manager Durocher rushed angrily from the coaching box to give Bithorn a piece of his mind. The Chicago pitcher reared back and hurled the ball at Durocher! Fortunately, he missed him. For his mad act, Bithorn drew a fine of $50. He insisted that the club pay it, but the Cubs refused.

When he declared that pitchers throw at hitters mainly on orders from the manager, he was brusquely told: "If you had hit Durocher, we'd have paid the fine. But you missed him. For that—pay it yourself!"

He did.

### ☞ THE EMPTY BARRELS THAT WON BASEBALL GAMES

John McGraw never missed a trick to win ball games. There was a time when he even made profitable use of the ancient superstition that the player who is lucky enough to see a truckload of empty barrels will make a bunch of base hits that day.

Many seasons ago the Giants and the Cubs were engaged in a bitter struggle for the pennant. Late in that campaign the teams clashed in an important four-game series that was to decide the pennant winner.

On the afternoon of the first game, just as the Giant players arrived at the ball park, an open truck piled high with empty barrels went rumbling down the street. Happy grins broke out on all the players' faces, as they roared with joy:

"What luck—empty barrels! That means we're going to get a lot of hits today!"

Inspired by this unfailing omen, the Giants buried the Cubs under a barrage of runs and won the initial encounter. The next day, another wagon-load of empty barrels passed by just as the Giants arrived at the ball park and were about to enter the clubhouse. Every day for four days, the New York

players saw a truckload of empty barrels pass by, and they swept the series and clinched the pennant.

After the fourth game and fourth consecutive victory, a wizened little man appeared in the Giants' clubhouse anxiously looking for McGraw.

"He isn't here now," said a player, "Can I help you?"

The timid little man piped up in a voice heard by all in the dressing room: "I want my dough. Mr. McGraw hired me to drive my wagon loaded with

empty barrels, and I've been driving past here every day now for four days and I ain't been paid yet!"

### ☞ IN THE SHADOW OF HIS DOOM

The immortal Walter Johnson, who threw faster than any pitcher who ever lived, never threw a ball at an enemy batter to scare him away from the plate. Yet, his speed terrified the mightiest sluggers.

One dark, windy day, Johnson faced the pennant-bound Cleveland Indians. In a late inning, Cleveland's star shortstop, Ray Chapman, came to bat. By that time it was so dark that it was almost impossible to see the ball. Ray Chapman took two fast strikes without removing his bat from his shoulder, then tossed his club away, and started back to the dugout.

"Wait a minute, Chapman," called out the umpire, "you've still got a strike coming to you!"

"Johnson can have it," replied Ray Chapman, "I don't want to take a chance and get killed by a pitched ball."

Ironically enough, a few days later, on a very sunny day, Ray Chapman was hit in the head by another pitcher—and killed.

### ☞ HE STOLE FIRST BASE

"Germany" Schaefer is the only baseball player to possess the unique distinction of having stolen first base. It happened while he was playing with the Detroit Tigers. He singled and stole second. Then, to everyone's surprise, he stole another base —only this time, just for a laugh, he retraced his steps, ran the wrong way, and stole first base! This stunt compelled the embarrassed lawmakers to write a rule into the books forbidding any ballplayer to steal first.

*BABE RUTH—*

*HE WALKED AMONG ALL PEOPLE*

## ☛ BABE RUTH

As long as ballplayers hit home runs, Babe Ruth will be remembered. The Sultan of Swat was the greatest of all sluggers. He hit 60 in one season, and 714 during his entire career.

As long as pitchers hurl scoreless world-series games, Babe Ruth will be remembered. He pitched 29 consecutive runless innings in world-series play.

He was a man who started life unwanted—a kid from the slums whose playground was his father's saloon. As a homeless boy, he roamed the streets of Baltimore, until he found asylum in an orphanage. From there Babe Ruth went on to become the most famous ballplayer in the world, and one of the game's most loved celebrities. The Babe earned a fortune of $2,000,000. But he gave baseball more than he took from it. It was the Sultan of Swat who saved the national pastime after the 1919 world-series gambling scandal. It was he who became a hero for millions of boys the world over. It was he who became an American institution. He is a legend in the heart of America, and, as long as the game is played, people will talk and tell stories of the one and only Babe Ruth.

## ☞ WHAT'S IN A NAME?

George Herman Ruth came by his nickname "Babe" in a curious way. When Jack Dunn, the owner-manager of the Baltimore Orioles, signed Ruth to his first job in professional baseball, he also acquired a son. Ruth had no parents, and Dunn had to file adoption papers to get the boy out of the Baltimore orphanage.

On joining the Baltimore club as a pitcher, the youngster was the victim of some rough hazing by veteran Oriole players.

One morning, the coach gathered the team in the clubhouse and warned them: "Fellows, you'll have to stop being rough with the new pitcher. He is Jack Dunn's babe, and if Dunn gets wind of this rough-housing, he won't like it. Go easy."

From that moment on, Ruth's nickname was "Babe."

## ☞ EXCUSE MY IGNORANCE

Long before Babe Ruth became the greatest home-run slugger in history, he won fame as a pitcher. But his first day as a hurler was almost his last.

Babe Ruth made his debut in pro ball when he

took the mound for the Baltimore Orioles. His catcher that day was Ben Egan.

As Babe Ruth went to the mound, Egan said, "Now don't be nervous, Babe, just watch me for the signals—two fingers for a fast ball, three fingers for a curve ball, and an open hand for a waste ball."

The Babe nodded. For seven innings he did fine. Then came the eighth, and the young pitcher found himself in trouble. The bases were full, with a heavy hitter at bat.

Again, the veteran catcher said to him, "Now don't be nervous Babe, remember my signals—two fingers for a fast ball, three for a curve, and an open hand for a waste ball."

The first pitch was a curve for a called strike. So was the second. However, the enemy runner on third was taking a long lead, and Egan signaled for a waste ball, to trap the runner off base. Ruth promptly cut the plate with a fast ball down the middle, and the batter belted it for a homer that won the game.

"You numskull," screamed Egan, "I signaled for a *waste* ball and you threw one right down the middle. You're lousy. Can't even follow signs!"

"What's griping you, sorehead?" barked Ruth. "I did just what you told me. When I saw you signal with an open hand I put it right where you wanted it—across his *waist!*"

### ☞  HIS PAJAMAS WERE SHOWING

One spring training season, Babe Ruth
flouted camp rules so flagrantly that the big boss of
the Yankees hired a detective to spy on him. Ruth
would often sneak out of the hotel when the ballplayers were supposed to be asleep, and make his
rounds. Ed Barrow wanted to catch the Babe—red-
handed. He instructed the private detective to
call him immediately upon Babe Ruth's return,
regardless of the hour.

It was about five o'clock one spring morning when
the peeper awakened Barrow to inform him that
Babe Ruth had just pulled in. The sleepy-eyed baseball boss slipped into a dressing robe and angrily
shuffled off to the player's room to confront him.
He threw open the door and there was Babe Ruth
in bed, with the bed sheets pulled up to his chin.
There was just one thing wrong with that picture.
Ruth was puffing on a big cigar.

"Isn't it an odd hour to be smoking?" thundered
Ed Barrow.

With boyish innocence, the Babe replied, "I

couldn't sleep very well. So I thought it might do me good to grab a smoke."

Whereupon Barrow snatched the covers off. Babe Ruth was fully dressed, even to his shoes.

For a moment, there was silence, and then, with a sheepish grin on his face, Babe Ruth said, "It's cold in the room, and I thought I'd slip on something to keep warm."

Even Barrow had to chuckle at the explanation.

### ☞ MEET MY BEST FRIENDS

The moon-faced guy with the massive shoulders, the spindly legs, and the heart-warming grin was everyone's friend, although there were times when he couldn't remember the names of his own teammates.

Babe brought his friend Paul Whiteman, the famous orchestra leader, to the Yankees' dugout. Whiteman wanted the thrill of personally meeting the stars of that mighty 1927 team, probably the greatest of all time. Babe started presenting his teammates to the musician, identifying them by the colorful nicknames he had for each. Player after player was introduced as "horse face," "apple head," "rabbit ears," "whiffy" and "loud mouth." In a daze, Whiteman followed Babe Ruth down the Yankee bench, meeting all the stars without learning the real name of a single player.

## ☞ BABE HAD A TANTRUM

Almost everything that Babe Ruth did as a player, even when he had his bad moments, helped make history. The good-natured Babe was never an umpire baiter, but there was a time when he lost his temper and socked a man in blue.

One June day in 1917, when Ruth was a pitcher for the Boston Red Sox, he took the mound against the Washington Senators. Brick Owens was the umpire behind the plate.

With the first ball Ruth pitched to the lead-off man, he found fault with the umpire's decisions.

"That was a strike, that first one was right over the plate!" an angry Babe roared at the umpire. "Another call like that one and I'll bust you one on the jaw."

Ruth wound up and pitched again, but Owens again called it a ball. Blazing with anger, the Babe deserted the mound, rushed toward home plate, and without further ceremony socked umpire Brick Owens just as he had promised. Promptly he was thrown out of the game.

The odd turn of this little story is that when Babe Ruth was thumbed out of the game, his roommate, Ernie Shore, relieved him on the mound and proceeded to make history. He retired 27 batters in a row—to pitch a perfect no-hit game.

### ☞ THE BOY BABE RUTH IGNORED

When he was just a shy boy of seventeen, he was taken to Wrigley Field in Los Angeles for the greatest event in his life—to shake the hand of Babe Ruth. At the time, baseball's mightiest slugger was working in a motion picture. Just as "The Great Man" limbered up his swing for the cameras, the shy boy was pushed forward and introduced to him. Annoyed by the interruption and preoccupied with his labors as a movie actor, Babe Ruth ignored the youngster as he mumbled, "Nice to know you, kid."

If that youngster of seventeen had been hurt by Babe Ruth's curt reception, he didn't show it. For him, it was an event of a lifetime. It is strange that the boy Babe Ruth ignored, years later became the greatest home-run hitter in the game—the player most likely to break Ruth's record of 60 home runs in one season. For the name of that boy was Ralph Kiner.

### ☞ BROTHER PAUL

Many years ago, Brother Paul was the superintendent of St. Mary's Industrial School of Baltimore, an institution for homeless and incorrigible boys. For almost two decades, Brother Paul supervised and guided the upbringing of children, and with his wisdom, kindness, and understanding, he helped mold them into useful citizens.

One day, during Brother Paul's tenure at that institution, there came to St. Mary's Industrial School a young hoodlum from the slum streets of Baltimore. He was a husky lad who defied all discipline and seemed to have no purpose in life except to start trouble. They tried to teach that youngster a useful trade, but he was not interested. None of the teachers at St. Mary's could cope with him until Brother Paul took a hand.

With infinite patience, Brother Paul tamed the boy and won his friendship. When Brother Paul discovered that the boy was interested in playing baseball, he encouraged him. It was Brother Paul who converted him from a left-handed catcher to a pitcher. As time passed and the boy grew older, Brother Paul realized that he possessed a marked talent, so he took him to an old baseball friend to ask for a job. Brother Paul's friend happened to be Jack Dunn, owner-manager of the Baltimore Orioles. Jack Dunn hired Brother Paul's protégé for $600 a season. To be sure that the orphan would have proper guidance, Brother Paul persuaded the owner of the Oriole team to adopt him. The lad Brother Paul put into professional baseball was George Herman Ruth!

As the years passed and great fame and fortune came to the Babe, the mighty "Sultan of Swat" remained Brother Paul's boy from St. Mary's School. Whenever things went wrong with Ruth, he always sought the understanding and the inspiration of Brother Paul, and Brother Paul was always there to help.

In the baseball season of 1927, the mighty Babe fell into a bad batting slump. He became despondent. His confidence was badly shaken. When Brother Paul heard about it, he packed a bag and made a hurried trip to New York. He spent several days with the Babe, talking to him. When Brother Paul left, the famous slugger came out of his slump with such violence that he hit 60 home runs that season, to set a record that has stood for many years, and may continue to stand forever!

☞ **HE CALLED HIS SHOT**

Babe Ruth holds more records than any man who played the game of baseball. During his twenty-two fabulous years in the major leagues, the immortal "King of Swat" hit an amazing total of 714 home runs. No four-base clout ever gave Babe Ruth a greater thrill than the home run he slugged on the afternoon of October 1, 1938, at Wrigley Field, Chicago.

It was more than a home run of typical Ruthian proportions; it was a home run that established Babe Ruth as the mightiest slugger of all time. With one haughty gesture he silenced the baseball crowd, then, at his will, prodded a hostile mob into frenzied cheers and tribute.

It was the third game of the world series between the Yankees and the Cubs. The Chicago ball park was jammed with some 50,000 home-town rooters. They were in an ugly and restless mood. In the first two games of that October classic, the "Bronx Bombers," sparked by Ruth, had demolished their opponent with mighty slugging. The Cubs now had to take that third game to preserve even a chance of winning the series. But there was the hulking Babe Ruth darkening their path. No wonder the Chicago players and home-town rooters hated that moon-

faced, homely, grinning giant. To add fuel to this
hate, before that world series began, Babe Ruth had
talked too much. In public print he had said harsh
things about the miserly Chicago club.

Hence, on that historic afternoon, the Chicago
fans came to the ball park to bury the "King of
Swat," not to praise him. On his first appearance at
the plate, 50,000 voices razzed him to the skies. But
Babe Ruth grinned arrogantly and with his first
swing of the game, in the very first inning, he sent
his team away to a 3-run lead with a homer into the
right-field bleachers.

Inning by inning, the desperate Cubs hacked away
at the Yankees' lead. By the start of the fifth, the
home-town team was only one run behind. Hopes
for a victory were again high in spite of Babe Ruth
and his murderous bat.

When the Babe came to bat in the fifth inning,
Earl Combs was on base. A violent verbal blast
greeted the Babe. It soon grew into the most hostile demonstration ever accorded a visiting baseball
player in Chicago history. Many stood up and cursed
him. Some shrieked filthy oaths. Others threw rot-
ten fruit. It was a strange and shocking attack upon
baseball's most famous home-run slugger, known
and loved throughout the world.

That demonstration of hate cut deep. It goaded
Babe Ruth into a gesture of contempt. For as the
Chicago pitcher, Charley Root, set himself to throw
his first pitch, Babe Ruth deliberately pointed to
the bleachers out in deep center field. Unmistak-

Rea Pri

ably, he was signaling to the hostile crowd where he planned to hit his next home run.

For a moment, the Chicago rooters were frozen into silence by the incredible arrogance of the man. Then the hostile crowd exploded again, more violently than before.

Charley Root threw one across the heart of the plate, but Babe Ruth let it pass. Before the umpire could call it a strike, which it was, Ruth grinned, raised his right hand, put up a finger, and called: "Strike one!"

The Cub hurler threw another fast ball through the middle. Again Babe Ruth stepped back, held up two fingers, and bawled: "Strike two!"

The next two pitches were very wide, and Babe Ruth laughed in derision as he let them float by. Now the count was 2 and 2. What would Charley Root throw? What would the Babe do now? The crowd was tense with expectation. However, lest the home-town rooters forget his boast, again Babe Ruth pointed his finger to the bleacher stands. The gesture set off a new explosion of raspberries, oaths, and insults. A lemon came flying through the air and landed at Ruth's feet. The crowd hooted raucously. Babe merely gripped his bat tighter and waited for the next pitch. It came! It was a hard fast ball, traveling to the plate on the wings of a perfect strike.

The Babe swung at it with all the power of his giant body. The ball never reached the catcher. It went soaring away, on and on, until it finally fell far up in the center-field bleachers, almost at the very spot to which Ruth had pointed. Babe Ruth had "called his shot" with one of the longest home runs he ever hit!

As Ruth jogged around the bases, the huge hostile crowd of Chicago rooters rose to its collective feet and cheered him as he had never been cheered before. The rabble was now paying homage to a King who could do no wrong!

There was another time when the Babe "called his shot" for one of the saddest of baseball occasions.

In the closing years of his life, almost everyone was aware he had become a tragic victim of cancer, but he himself did not know. Although bedridden by his illness and tortured by pain, the weary Bambino believed he would lick the trouble which had forced him to the side lines. However, on the evening of August 16, 1948, when his nurse came into his hospital room, she was startled to see the sick Babe Ruth standing on his feet and trying to walk across the room. Shocked, she asked him where he was going.

The Babe smiled sadly and replied, "I'm going over the valley."

Those were the last words Babe Ruth ever spoke, for he went into a deep coma, and an hour later he was dead.

The first world series ever played actually took place as far back as 1860. It ended in violence and bloodshed, without determining a baseball champion.

In 1860, there were many ball teams playing throughout the United States. But the two accepted as the best in the game, were the Excelsiors and the Atlantics—both from Brooklyn.

After the Excelsiors had completed a successful tour of the country, they challenged the Atlantics to a postseason series of three games. The challenge was accepted, and that first world series was to be at the home grounds of the Atlantics.

The Excelsiors took the first game, but the Atlantics won the second. Interest and excitement became so intense that 5,000 people turned out to see the deciding game. The crowd consisted largely of hoodlums and notorious bad men of that day, as well as gamblers who had wagered heavily on the Atlantics to win.

From the first inning, fights began to break out all over the ball park. But cooler heads quelled the disturbances, so that the game could continue. When the Excelsiors took an early lead, disorder again broke out, and the tough element became unmanageable.

At the end of the sixth inning, the Excelsiors were leading 8 to 6. The gamblers and the hoodlums went to work to save the game for their favorite team. They invaded the field with knives, sticks, and stones, and started a wild free-for-all.

Players were beaten, and the more timid spectators were frightened from the ball park. The police were helpless to stop the riot. It was impossible to continue the game. After a hurried conference between the captains of both teams, the game was called off, and the first world series ever played was declared a draw.

### 🔲 IT HAPPENED DOWN MEXICO WAY

In 1917, when the Chicago White Sox were to play the Giants in a world series, Mexico was embroiled in revolution. The bandit chief, Pancho Villa, spearheaded the uprising. Covering his stormy activities for the American press was Norman Walker, an ex-ballplayer. This American foreign correspondent became a trusted friend of the notorious and feared Pancho Villa.

Before launching an assault on a Mexican city, Villa called in his American reporter friend and confided the date of his planned attack. Aware that Villa was headline-happy, the American correspondent pointed out that the battle would not attract page-one attention in the United States newspapers. Since a world series was starting at the same time, baseball would overshadow any war news.

So Pancho Villa postponed this military action for seven days. Annoyed by the long wait, he finally abandoned his campaign against that Mexican city. Thus, a world series spared a city and saved hundreds of people from possible death.

### ☞ STRANGEST OF ALL WORLD SERIES

As every fan knows, when a baseball season officially ends, the pennant winner of the National League meets the pennant winner of the American League for the baseball championship.

However, two major-league teams actually played for the championship not at the end of a pennant campaign but before the official baseball season started!

In 1885, the two major circuits were the National

League and the American Association. At that time, the Chicago White Stockings and the St. Louis Browns were the best clubs in their respective loops. The Browns won the American Association pennant, and the White Stockings finished first in the National League. At the conclusion of the 1885 baseball season, the two clubs met in a world-series contest. But of the seven games played, each team won three and one contest ended in a tie.

So the rival-league teams called it a draw and went home for the winter. Toward the close of the following season when it became evident that the same teams would triumph again, Chris Von Der Ahe of the Browns challenged Albert Spalding, the owner of the White Stockings, to another series to be played at the end of the 1886 baseball season. Magnate Spalding had little desire to pit his club against the Browns. To discourage a world-series contest, he made the daring suggestion that the teams meet on a basis of winner-take-all. Chris Von Der Ahe quickly and happily accepted the proposition. So, at the end of that season, the Browns played Chicago in a world series—winner to take all gate receipts. The Browns gave the White Stockings a sound licking, racking up four straight games to cop that world series. The "gate" amounted to about $20,000—big money in those days.

His humiliating defeat and the loss of all that world-series cash rankled deep in the heart of club owner Albert Spalding. He promptly issued a challenge for another series, again for the championship of the world. It was agreed that the teams would play in April, 1887, before the regular league schedules got under way.

And so, in 1887, the strangest of all world series was played between St. Louis and Chicago. It was a perfectly legitimate contest, but it took place not at the end of a baseball year but before the season had even begun. Chicago won this time—4 games to 2.

### ☞ THE REVOLT OF THE IVORY SLAVES

There was once a "sit-down" players' strike in the world series. It happened in 1918. The Chicago Cubs played the Boston Red Sox. The first four games failed to draw at the gate. The players realized that they would come out of the classic with very little prize money, so they refused to come out on the field for the fifth game. A committee representing the players of both teams argued with Ban Johnson, then the Czar of Baseball. Finally, they consented to play out the rest of that world series. It was the first, last, and only "sit-down" players' strike in baseball!

### ☞ WARNING—PITCHER TO BE MURDERED

A pitcher once hurled in a world series even though he had been warned that if he dared play, he would be murdered.

The Detroit Tigers had a sensational rookie pitcher known to baseball fame as "Schoolboy" Rowe. In his first year in the big leagues, he blazed his way up the glory trail with 24 victories and hurled the Tigers into the world series with the St. Louis Cardinals. A day before the opening game, his sister was shopping on Main Street when a note was slipped into her hand. It was an unsigned threat that read:

"Schoolboy will never pitch more than one ball in the world series. We'll get him if he does. St. Louis must win!"

The threat was ignored, but that night "Schoolboy" Rowe received another note, through the mails, threatening his life.

It was soon revealed that other unsigned letters had arrived, delivered to the club owner and the team manager, all threatening Rowe's life if he dared pitch. A bodyguard of police were assigned to protect "Schoolboy" Rowe. Detectives slept outside his door, went to the clubhouse with him, and mingled with the crowds.

"Schoolboy" Rowe pitched in that world series— and won his game! It was the only time on record when a pitcher needed police protection to hurl in a world series!

## ☞ THE COCKY NOBODY

In 1909, when the Pirates won the pennant, Babe Adams was an obscure rookie pitcher who had come from a sleepy Missouri town with a population of less than 150 people. Pittsburgh was to face a mighty Detroit club in the world series, led by Ty Cobb, the greatest ballplayer of all time, and assisted by some of baseball's most famous sluggers.

Before the first game, Adams was sitting on the bench watching Detroit's batting practice. He panicked the Pirates' bench with laughter as he loudly exclaimed: "Gee, I wish manager Clarke would pitch me. I'd stand those fellows on their heads. Cobb and the rest of those Tigers look like suckers to me!"

Then suddenly, Clarke threw a shiny new ball to rookie Babe Adams, and snapped, "You're in, Babe! Go on out there and pitch!"

Babe Adams thought he was being kidded at first. But when he realized that destiny had chosen him to be the first rookie pitcher to start a world series opener, he went out and won. Three games he pitched in that world series, and he won three times!

### ☛ THE WOULD-BE WORLD-SERIES HERO

Tom Clarke waited a long time to play in a world series. He was a catcher who had knocked around the majors, always dreaming of the day he would play in a world series. The years passed. Tom Clarke grew older, and his career as an active player neared its close. But in his heart still blazed the dream that someday, somehow, someway, he would appear in a series.

In 1918, Clarke was a second-string catcher with the Cubs when they won the pennant and the right to play the Boston Red Sox for the baseball crown.

But as that world series progressed, Clarke's dream began to fade, inning by inning, and game by game. He rode the bench while Bill Killefer, the regular Chicago catcher, played every game.

Tom Clarke's heart was heavy with disappointment. All these years he had waited so patiently. Now Fate was robbing him of his chance of making at least one appearance in world-series play.

The last game of that classic was almost over. It was the ninth inning. The score was Boston 3, Chicago 2. The Cubs rallied. Two men were on, with one out. Up to bat came a pinch hitter for catcher Killefer. As that pinch hitter went to the plate, there also came a call for Tom Clarke. Manager Fred Mitchell snapped at him: "Grab a bat and be ready to hit for Douglas!"

Tom Clarke could hardly believe his ears. The manager had told him to be ready to hit for the Chicago pitcher, Shufflin' Phil Douglas. Since only one man was out, that meant that Clarke would be the next batter. At last his dream had come true.

Eagerly, he picked up a bat and went out on the field to await his turn. Suddenly, he thought of his wife sitting in a field box near the Chicago dugout. Tom Clarke turned, grinned, and waved at her as if to say: "Look, honey! At last I'm in a world-series game. Watch me do my stuff!"

While he was waving to his wife, with his back toward the diamond, there was a sharp crack of bat against ball. Clarke turned quickly, took one look at what had happened, and fainted. For the Chicago batter had hit into a double play and the game was over!

Everything went black for Tom Clarke. He was in a stupefied daze, unable to tell what was happening around him. For that double play marked for him not only the end of the game, but the end of the world!

His manager, his teammates, his wife and doctors, all tried to bring Tom out of his stupor. But for days none succeeded. The curious twist to this story is that the double play which finished that game was not the official end of that series. It was actually the end of the fourth game, and it took two more games for the Red Sox to lick the Cubs. But Tom Clarke never knew it. The shock of that double play completely blotted out his memory, and for many years he labored under the strange delusion that the twin killing had ended that classic and robbed him of his one and only chance to play in a world series!

### ☛ THE PIGEON THAT STOLE THE SHOW

In the 1933 world series, the New York Giants played the Washington Senators. Three of the games were played at Griffith Stadium in Washington.

Every afternoon, just before the game was to start, a little blue pigeon appeared mysteriously and hunted worms. The players, the umpires, the groundskeepers, tried to shoo that pigeon away, but

all failed. It continued to come back, to the identical spot, calmly grubbing for worms in the infield. Finally, play went on. But everybody in that crowded ball park, including the President of the United States, watched that little pigeon for three days, wandering around the infield, an uninvited guest at the series.


## THEN CAME THE RAINS

There was a time when a torrent almost washed out a world series and touched off a bitter feud that nearly wrecked relations between the American and National Leagues.

In the world series of 1911 between the Giants and Athletics, play alternated from the Polo Grounds in New York to Shibe Park in Philadelphia. On the eve of the first game, there was a downpour. But the teams played the two days following. In the third game, Buck Herzog, the Giants' tough second baseman, accidentally spiked the Philadelphia idol, "Home-Run" Baker.

That spiking incident might have been forgotten except that no game was played on the following day. It had begun to rain again. Then came the longest break in the history of the series. It rained for six consecutive days.

On the first rainy day, the baseball reporters found themselves with nothing interesting to write about, and used the spiking incident as a lead. In blazing headlines, appeared charges by the Athletics that the Giants played "dirty ball."

On the second day of rain, newspaper stories credited the gentle, soft-spoken Philadelphia manager, Connie Mack, with strong remarks about Buck Herzog's rough playing.

On the third day of rain, John McGraw popped off in the newspapers, attacking Connie Mack.

On the fourth day of rain, Ban Johnson, the President of the American League, made a violent public statement that branded the Giants a gang of hoodlums and rowdies.

On the fifth day of rain, Thomas Lynch, the President of the National League, took up the defense of his circuit, McGraw, and the Giants.

Now accusations and counter charges flooded the newspapers. Sides were sharply drawn for war between the leagues.

On the sixth day of rain, Charlie Ebbets, owner of the Brooklyn Dodgers, came out and appealed for an armistice.

"Let us be reasonable," he pleaded. "This will not only end the world series but ruin the game permanently."

After six continuous days of rain, Providence took a hand. The weather cleared, play was resumed.

It took almost two weeks to end that memorable world series, with its ominous burden of feeling between players, team managers, club owners, and league officials. The six days of rain also had dire consequences for the reporters. Many who had arrived with ample expense money lost it in the nightly poker games. Some writers soon ran out of funds and wound up living in cheap boarding-houses. All but a few went home broke, anxious to forget the bitter memory of that long-drawn-out world series—a series which will never be forgotten in the legends of baseball.

### ☞ IT WAS FOR HIS PAPPY

In 1940, Bucky "Bobo" Newsom, helped pitch the Detroit Tigers to a pennant. Before the start of the world series, "Bobo" received word that his father was dead. Bobo and his dad had been pals, and the pitcher was heartbroken.

Minutes before he was to pitch the opener, Bobo faced his teammates and said, "I'm going to pitch this game and I'm going to win. If any of you mess it up for me, I'll beat you up—for this one I've got to win for my pappy."

"Bobo" scored his victory. He took a second game in that world series, in memory of his departed dad, and he came close to winning a third.

### ☞ IN MEMORIUM

Robert Cooper was a humble rural mail carrier in Atherton, Missouri. He taught two of his sons to play baseball and lived long enough to see his boys become famous major-league stars: one, the best catcher of his time; the other, a leading pitcher. In 1943 the St. Louis Cardinals played the Yankees in the world series. Morton Cooper was assigned to hurl the second game. An hour before the game, the Cooper boys learned that their father had passed away. Pitcher Morton Cooper was heartbroken, but he refused to give up his assignment. With his brother Walker behind the plate, Morton Cooper pitched and scored a victory.

### 🐾 MAMA'S BOY

In the 1935 world series between Detroit and the Chicago Cubs, shortly before he was to pitch, Alvin Crowder was informed that his mother had suddenly died. Although grief-stricken, the "Old General" took the hill and pitched one of the greatest games in world-series history.

### 🐾 TO THE RESCUE

In 1940, Cincinnati won the pennant. That year, the Reds had a player named Billy Myers, a shortstop. Six days before the world series, Myers quit the team. He was moody, refused to play ball anymore, and disappeared. After a frantic search, the missing shortstop was located. A club official made connections with Billy Myers in his hide-out and talked to him on the telephone. He threatened to have him barred from baseball for life if he failed to return at once. Billy did, and he played in the world series. The pay-off was that Myers drove in the winning run in the seventh and deciding game.

### ☞ THE GALS HAD THE LAST WORD

It happened back in 1906 when the legendary "Hitless Wonders," the Chicago White Sox, played the Chicago Cubs for the world championship. Chicago went mad with excitement. Business establishments closed, thousands of people stayed away from work, and the Mayor of Chicago actually declared world series time a legal city holiday. Chicago never had known anything like it. Thousands stormed locked gates, trying to squeeze their way into a ball park jammed to the rafters with people.

In that world series, the "Hitless Wonders" surprised the baseball world and toppled the Cubs, then hailed as baseball's mightiest team. When the final game was over and the White Sox were champions, the triumphant players ran from the field to escape the mob that poured out of the stands to pay them homage. The victory-mad crowd, balked in its purpose, surrounded the field box where sat the wives of the White Sox players, and demanded that the wife of each of the nine Chicago regulars make a speech. It was the first, last, and only time that women launched into an orgy of oratory as a finale to a world series.

## ☛ A SHOWER FOR A BALLPLAYER

Once a shower of fruit and garbage actually drove a star player out of a world-series contest. It happened in 1934 when the Cardinals played Detroit. The Cards were in Detroit for the final game of the classic. On a close play at third, Joe Medwick, the Cards' best slugger, roughed up Detroit's third baseman. When Joe Medwick returned to his outfield position, the enraged Detroit fans fired a barrage of fruit and pop bottles at Medwick's head. For several minutes, it rained garbage in left field. Policemen tried to stop it but all in vain. After half an hour, Judge Landis, then czar of baseball, ordered Joe Medwick taken out so that the world series game could be finished.

## ☛ THE COSTLY HANDSHAKE

In the 1934 world series, the Detroit Tigers needed but one more victory to beat St. Louis. Their star pitcher, "Schoolboy" Rowe, was primed for that game. He had beaten the Cards once in that series, and he was a good bet to repeat. However, on the eve of the sixth game, he was invited to appear on a radio program. After his stint on the air, he met the motion-picture comedian, Joe E. Brown, who shook his hand vigorously to wish him luck.

Pitcher Rowe returned the handshake with a bone-crushing grip. One squeeze led to another, and the pitcher and the movie star began to test their respective strengths. As a result, the fingers of Rowe's hand became so bruised that, when it came time for him to pitch in the sixth game of that world series, he could hardly hold the ball. He lost the game. The Cardinals won and went on to win the world series. A "handshake" had cost a team a championship.

### 🐾 DOOMED MEN OF GLORY

Time has woven strange and unhappy
stories around many world-series heroes, an un-
comfortable number of whom have been doomed
men.

The first great series hero was Christy Mathewson.
In the 1905 classic he pitched and won three games
—all by shutouts. The fabulous "Big Six" of the
pitching mound died before his time, a victim of
tuberculosis.

The next great world-series hero was a third baseman named George Rohe. He was an unexpected
performer, for when the 1906 classic started, he was
just a utility infielder for the Chicago White Sox.
But when it ended, George Rohe was the glory boy!
Some years afterward, as an unwanted ballplayer
toiling in the obscurity of the bushes, George Rohe
mysteriously disappeared and was never heard of
again!

In 1907 Claude Rossman was a utility first base-
men with the Detroit Tigers. Rossman emerged from
this classic as its batting champion! However, he too
was fated for doom, for he died in an insane asylum.

"From Tinker-to-Evers-to-Chance." Who'll ever
forget the legend of that trio? Not once, but four
times they won laurels in world championships.
However, time doomed each of them. Little Johnny
Evers had to live imprisoned in a wheel chair for

many years before merciful death ended his agony. Joe Tinker lost all his money, two wives, and a leg before death wrote finish to his story. And Frank Chance, the giant first baseman, once the strongest man in baseball, was a human skeleton of less than 90 pounds before tuberculosis finally snuffed out his life and ended his misery.

The brightest star of 1913 was a hulking giant named Larry McLean. He not only emerged from that classic as a great catcher but also led the hitters. As a series hero, he too was doomed to an untimely end, for some years later Larry McLean was killed in a barroom brawl.

In 1918 Charley Hollocher, shortstop for the Chicago Cubs, was baseball's "man of the hour." But with baseball fame and fortune his for the taking, Hollocher suddenly left the game to protect his health. Years later, he was found on a deserted street —mysteriously murdered!

The hero of the 1919 world series, judging by all records, was a White Sox outfielder who led both teams with a healthy .375 batting average. He hit the only home run of that series, handled 30 chances in the outfield without an error, and threw out 5 men at home plate. Yet, because of his playing in that same world series, that White Sox outfielder was banished from organized baseball for the rest of his life! He was the tragic "Shoeless" Joe Jackson, accused with his "Black Sox" teammates of conspiring to throw that world series.

There never was a more dramatic world-series hero

than Grover Cleveland Alexander. It was in the 1926 series when grizzled Old Pete Alexander fashioned imperishable history as he struck out Tony Lazzeri with the bases full, to win the classic for the St. Louis Cardinals. But fate also doomed Alexander to a tragic end. The last years of his life were spent in misery as he wandered the earth—neglected, forgotten, and broke. For a time, he even exhibited himself as a "freak" in a penny-arcade flea circus. Finally, he died, a victim of cancer.

The brightest hero of the 1936 world series was an outfielder named Jake Powell. Playing for the star-studded Yankees, it was this substitute who emerged as the hero and batting champion of that series. But years later, he killed himself!

"Iron Horse" Lou Gehrig, the immortal Yankee first baseman, was also a world-series hero. He wound up paralyzed, victim of a dread disease that snuffed out his life at thirty-eight.

Babe Ruth was a world-series hero in several classics. He too died before his time, a tragic victim of cancer.

Hugh Casey, one of the greatest relief pitchers in history, was also a world-series hero. In the 1947 classic he pitched in six of the seven games played by the Brooklyn Dodgers—a record that still stands! He also holds a record of winning a world-series game with one pitch. Some years later, he shot and killed himself.

World series heroes! Their glory is brief, although their names may linger long in memory.

# UMPIRES
## ARE ALSO PEOPLE ☞

## ☞ SO CHARMED TO MEET YOU

Harry "Steamboat" Johnson, once the most colorful of all minor-league umpires, was assigned to work a game in New Orleans. It was the first Ladies' Day game ever played in that city. When Steamboat Johnson came out on the field, the female guests stood up in a body and shrilly jeered him.

Somewhat hurt, the famous umpire walked up close to the grandstand, faced the mob of hooting women, and shouted in a high falsetto: "Why, girls, I don't think we've been properly introduced."

"Well, we have now!" boomed the voice of a huge woman in the stands. She leaned over the grandstand rail and broke her parasol over Steamboat Johnson's head.

## ☞ ROW FOR YOUR LIFE

Tommy Connolly is famous for officiating in the first American League game in history, played on April 24, 1901. He almost lost his life as an umpire. He started his career in the New York State League. One afternoon he called one against the

Albany club. His decision so infuriated the partisan fans that they actually tried to lynch him. They chased umpire Connolly into the clubhouse where he barricaded himself to save his neck. The frightened umpire did not leave until night had fallen. He crawled to the near-by banks of the Hudson River and, under the cover of darkness, escaped in a rowboat. He lived to compile the staggering record of fifty-eight years of officiating in organized baseball.

### ☞ NOT WITHOUT DANGER

It may be hard to believe, but there have been two occasions in baseball history when an umpire's life was the price of a decision.

In 1899, two professional clubs played a game at Lowndesborough, Alabama. The umpire was Samuel White. All that afternoon, White took abuse from both teams. In a late inning, after he had called a close one, a player rushed at him hurling violent threats. Umpire Sam White knocked the man down. Whereupon, the ballplayer grabbed a bat and brought it down on the umpire's head—and killed him!

Shocking as that tragedy was, it was repeated a few years later in a game played in Indiana. There, an umpire named Ora Jennings got into an argument with a player who struck him on the head with a bat—and killed him!

### 🖙 STAY OUT OF MY BALL PARK

One afternoon in 1901, the Chicago Cubs played the Giants at the Polo Grounds. It was a tense battle. Umpire Nash ordered three Giants out of that game.

Sitting in the stands that afternoon was the millionaire Andrew Freedman, Giants' owner. He was the most bellicose magnate who ever ran the destinies of a major-league ball club. Freedman became so furious when Nash banished three of his best players that he had to be restrained from rushing out on the field to assault the umpire.

In his rage, he announced that he would not permit Nash to umpire any future Giants games, and that never as long as he was owner of the club would he let Nash into the Giants' park.

Umpire Nash was assigned to officiate at the next game, but when he came to the ball park, he was refused admission. Freedman had posted extra guards to keep the umpire out. And as long as Andrew Freedman remained owner of the Giants, Nash was not permitted to set foot inside the New York ball park.

### 🖙 DON'T WRITE

Bill Klem, who never denied he was the greatest umpire in baseball history, once wrote a story for a national magazine. He said:

"An umpire who is on the job should never be hit by a batted ball."

On the day that magazine story appeared, Bill Klem was umpiring a game. Naturally it was at Ebbets Field. And of course he was solidly smacked by a batted ball.

☞ **AN UMPIRE WHO THOUGHT HE WAS PAUL REVERE**

"Riding an umpire" is as old as the game itself. But did you ever hear of the time an umpire actually did the riding?

It happened years ago, when Bill Summers was working the Eastern League. He was handling a series that was to decide a hot pennant race, and for the first game the partisan fans and home-town players "got on" him. All he heard was: "Hey, Jesse James, get a horse!"

That ancient and insulting bit of advice annoyed Honest Bill. The next day, on his way to the ball park, he spied a horse for hire. The umpire decided to make his hecklers look foolish, so he hired the horse. Fully dressed in chest protector and iron mask, Summers came riding into the ball park astride his nag. It panicked the crowd and the players as well. When Summers reached home plate, the horse suddenly reared and the umpire landed in a heap. He quickly jumped up, brushed himself off, turned to the howling mob, and shouted: "Jesse James has arrived! Play ball!"

## ☞ A LESSON IN GRAMMAR

In an important game, McGraw rushed up to umpire Bill Klem and screamed: "When are you going to learn the rules?"

"Seems to me, John," replied Bill calmly, "I learned you something about the rules last season!"

"You dumb ignoramus!" sneered McGraw, "You don't even know any grammar! Don't you know that you can't "learn" anything to anyone. You can teach someone but you can't learn him!"

"Mr. McGraw," replied Klem sadly shaking his head, "It looks as though I can neither teach you nor learn you anything. You're just hopeless—so maybe you better leave the game!"

And McGraw was thumbed out.

## ☞ LORD BYRON WAS A MAN FOR WORDS

Many years ago there was an umpire, Bill Byron by name. Because of his grand manner and fine voice, the fans and players nicknamed him "Lord" Byron. He would often sing out the balls and strikes so that he could be heard all over the ball park. Byron had a keen wit and revenged himself on nagging ballplayers, not with his fists but with his tongue.

At the time there was a conceited player by the name of Huttin. Huttin wasn't playing one day, but sat in the dugout riding Byron on every decision. Finally the ninth inning came, and the home team was three runs behind with a man on base. Huttin was ordered to bat for the pitcher. In those days, the umpire announced all substitutions to the fans. Lord Byron smiled, turned to the grandstand, and in his loudest and most melodious voice, shouted: "Huttin now hitting for nuthin'!"

That wisecrack threw the fans into an uproar and poor Huttin struck out. That's how one nimble umpire evened the score!

### WHEN LORD BYRON RAN OUT OF WORDS

One day, players and fans were riding Lord Byron. They made fun of his walk and imitated his sonorous voice. Finally, the arbiter couldn't stand it any more. He walked up to the stands and roared: "Listen you bums, cut out them personalities."

For a second there was a hush. Then, from the depth of the dugout, boomed the voice of a ballplayer: "C'mon Byron, cut out them grammar, and get back to work."

☞   **UMPIRE FOR A DAY**

Around the turn of the century, Patrick Casey was a fair player but never lucky enough to rise above the obscurity of the bushes. He became an umpire. For a time, "he called 'em as he saw 'em," and he was a happy man. But then he lost his job. The years passed, and the old umpire fell on evil times. Pat Casey drifted into trouble. There came a day when Casey knew that he was about to die. It was his "last wish" that he umpire just one more ball game. His plea was heeded. A special baseball game was arranged for him. It took place on an afternoon in the summer of 1911. Patrick Casey umpired. He gave a fine performance, for all through that game there wasn't a single complaint about any of his decisions. When that contest was over, the players of both teams shook his hand and told him what a good job he had done. It was the strangest demonstration of affection ever seen on a ball field between players and an umpire. Then, umpire Patrick Casey walked off the ball field, a contented man. The next day he was dead. He had been electrocuted. For Patrick Casey, who had umpired a baseball game as "a dying wish," was a convict in the Nevada State Penitentiary under sentence of death.

## ☛ IGNORANCE IS NO EXCUSE

Jimmy Dykes always believed certain umps were "out to get him." His particular tormentor was Bill McGowan. For the slightest cause, that ump would thumb tough little Dykes to the showers. One day, a teammate of Jimmy's was ejected by McGowan for using bad language. Dykes rushed up to McGowan intending to demand what his teammate had said to the ump. But before he even opened his mouth, Bill McGowan shouted at him:

"And you're out of the game, too, Dykes!"

"What for?"

"For expostulation!" answered McGowan.

"Nuts!" barked Jimmy Dykes, "You're just showing off. You don't even know what that word means."

"I don't eh," sneered McGowan, "Well, I do, Mr. Dykes. It means holding up the game!"

## ☛ A SQUELCH IN TIME

Bill Klem once squelched a ballplayer in this way. Pee Wee Reese, the famous Brooklyn shortstop, was at bat, and the beloved umpire was behind the plate. After a called strike, Pee Wee glared at Klem. The umpire shrugged his shoulders and said to him: "Young man, don't blame me. It was the pitcher who fooled you."

## ☞ WHEN HIS SHOE WAS ON THE OTHER FOOT

Probably the toughest umpire of all was Tim Hurst. He loved a battle, at even terms or against odds.

A tough ballplayer once forgot himself and hollered at Hurst: "If you didn't have that mask on I'd punch you on the nose."

Hurst quickly removed the mask and brought it right down on the ballplayer's head.

One summer day in Cincinnati, Tim Hurst dug his own grave as a National League umpire. The crowd was heckling him, and finally someone in the stands threw a beer stein at him. Hurst whirled, picked up the mug, and hurled it back into the crowd. It struck a fan and knocked him unconscious. The crowd leaped out of the stands and charged the umpire. But Hurst held his ground and for a few furious moments, fought the mob off single-handed. Police rescued him. At the end of the season, the league eased him out of the game. However, when it looked like Tim Hurst's finish, the owner of the old St. Louis Browns, Chris Von Der Ahe, came to his rescue and gave him a baseball job. He made Hurst manager of his St. Louis team. The club became the talk of the baseball world—for one day! For a day after he became manager, the old St. Louis ball park burned down. Then the St. Louis team went into a tailspin and continued to lose until the end of the season, finishing last in a twelve-club league. Needless to say, Tim Hurst was fired. But the odd part of umpire Tim Hurst's brief career as a manager was that he became the worst umpire baiter in the league.

### ☞ YOU CAN'T TRUST A BALLPLAYER

One hot afternoon Bill Klem was behind the plate in a tight game between the Dodgers and the Pirates. The bases were loaded, when George Grantham of the Bucs was called out on strikes. The player turned on Bill Klem: "Hell, Bill, you're blind. That ball was outside a mile."

Being in a good mood, Klem smilingly replied, "I'll leave it to the Dodger catcher, to say what it was."

Whereupon the Dodger catcher, Johnny Gooch, stood up and said with a sneer, "Alibi your own lousy decisions, I've got troubles of my own."

Bill turned on the catcher and bellowed: "Another word out of you, you fresh bum, and out of the game you go."

"I hope I do," replied catcher Gooch. "I've been trying to tell that dumb manager of mine, Robinson, that I've got a sore foot, but the fat old clown won't listen."

Bill Klem didn't kick Gooch out of the game.

## ☞ TURNABOUT IS FAIR PLAY

In 1906, in a game between the Giants and the Cubs, umpire Johnstone called out a Giant player on a close play. The player started a row, and the fans became so excited that they assaulted the umpire. The police rescued him. The next day, when the umpire arrived at the ball park, the gate-keeper refused to admit him. The Chicago team refused to play when John McGraw appointed one of his own players as umpire in place of the missing arbiter. So the would-be umpire promptly announced that the game had been forfeited to the Giants by a score of 9 to 0.

Meanwhile, outside the ballpark, Johnstone announced that he had forfeited the game to Chicago by a score of 9 to 0. The forfeit to Chicago stood, and Johnstone was assigned to the following day's game.

That morning, he was the most frightened man in the world. However, as he stepped out on the field, a thunderous roar went up from the crowded stands—a roar not of anger, but strangely enough, of approval. "Hurray for Johnstone!" yelled the crowd. The surprised umpire gratefully acknowledged the salute to his gameness. It was the strangest "turnabout" an umpire ever experienced.

### HE GAVE HIM AN EARFUL

During a world series, umpire Brick Owen squelched tough and witty Mickey Cochrane as no ballplayer had ever been silenced before. Cochrane, known for his big protruding ears, kept protesting Owen's decisions on balls and strikes. Finally, Owen snapped at him: "Mickey, if you would only pin back those big ears of yours, I could probably see the ball better."

### ☞ KNOW YOUR UNDERTAKER

About 1900, umpire Silk O'Loughlin became friends with a St. Louis undertaker named
Arthur Donnelly. Whenever O'Loughlin umpired
in St. Louis, the undertaker would drive him to the
ball park in one of his funeral hacks. Soon the
friendly mortician was providing this unusual service for all the arbiters who worked the St. Louis
games. He also wined and dined them. When the
undertaker died, he made a provision in his will for
the continuance of this free taxi service as long as
his undertaking firm remained in existence.

### ☞ LAUGH CLOWN LAUGH

The sensitivity of umpires is puzzling.
Big Jack Sheridan was working a game in Detroit.
It was being played on a Sunday, before Sunday
baseball was common in the major leagues. The late
J. T. Navin owned the Tigers at the time. He cau-
tioned his players to be on their best behavior that
day—particularly not to spout any profanity.

The lead-off man for Detroit was Davey Jones, an
outfielder. The first pitch was wide by almost a foot,
but Jack Sheridan called it a strike. Incensed, Jones
whirled on the umpire. He was about to let fly with
some choice words when he remembered the club

owner's strict instructions. So he simply gulped, and without uttering a word, he smiled at the ump. Sheridan, who had braced himself for the onslaught he expected, was bewildered by the player's silent reaction to his bum call.

"So, laugh at me, will you!" roared the ump. "Well, get off the field, ya nasty bum—you're out of the game!"

I'M TELLING YOU . . .

## 🖙 I'M TELLING YOU . . .

Baseball grounds were originally only village greens, unfenced and without seats. When the lady friends of the players became curious enough to attend, benches had to be provided, and thus the "grandstand" came into existence. The first enclosed baseball park was the Union Grounds in Brooklyn, built in 1862.

On August 27, 1894, the player who covered first base for the Boston Braves in a charity exhibition game was James J. Corbett, famed in boxing history as the heavyweight champion of the world. He also played baseball for the Paterson and Milwaukee clubs.

Jackie Jensen is the only ballplayer in history who played baseball in a world series and football in the Rose Bowl. In 1947, as an all-American fullback for U.S.C., he starred in the Rose Bowl with a 67-

yard touchdown run. A couple of years later, he played for the Yankees in the world series.

Sam Breadon started in the St. Louis Cardinals' baseball park as a peddler selling popcorn and wound up owning the ball club which he eventually sold for $3,500,000.

When the National League was first organized, the ballplayers were charged $30 for their uniforms and 50 cents a day for board away from home. Each club in the league was assessed an entrance fee of $100.

Earle "Greasy" Neale was the only player in baseball to star in the major leagues and then become a football coach successful enough to mastermind a college team to the Rose Bowl. He was an outfielder with the Cincinnati Reds and football coach of Washington and Jefferson University.

Bill Klem, acclaimed as the greatest umpire in baseball history, never played a single game in organized ball.

A. J. Reach was the first professional baseball player. He was the first ballplayer to be transferred from one city to another for cash, when Brooklyn sold him to the Philadelphia Athletics for $275. No professional ever equaled his record of scoring 34 runs in one day.

In the beginning nobody went to a baseball game, for the game was called "one old cat."

Until 1872, home plate was made out of iron. For the next fifteen years, stone was used, until the rubber home plate was finally introduced to baseball. But the other three bases were solid wooden posts, 4 feet high.

Ferris Fain, first baseman for the Philadelphia Athletics, is the only player in the major leagues whose father ever rode a horse in the Kentucky Derby. It happened on May 11, 1912.

Baseball gloves and masks were introduced for the first time in the season of 1875. The chest protector came into use in 1885. Chest protectors were first worn by catchers under the uniform to save them from being labeled sissies.

It was James Tyng, a catcher for the Harvard University baseball team, who, had the first inspiration for a catcher's mask. Dared by the captain of his team to catch standing close behind the plate, Tyng took a mask used in fencing to the local tinsmith and had the mesh ripped out and a thicker wide-spaced wiring put in to protect his face. Thus was originated the mask now universally used by catchers and umpires.

An accident to Arthur Irwin, shortstop of the Providence baseball club of 1883, led to the invention of the infielder's glove. Shortstop Irwin broke a finger on his left hand and, to be able to play in the next day's game, bought a buckskin driving glove several sizes too large for him and padded it to protect the bandage around his finger. In the next afternoon's game, he made such sensational stops that other infielders quickly borrowed the idea, and soon Arthur Irwin's infield glove was widely copied.

Undoubtedly the most fruitful year for rookies in major-league history was 1925. The rookies who started that year on the road to fame were: Mel Ott, Chick Hafey, Freddie Fitzsimmons, Charley Gehringer, "Lefty" Moses Grove, Charlie Ruffing, Mickey Cochrane, Jimmie Foxx, and Lou Gehrig.

The first box score appeared on July 5, 1853. It was Henry Chadwick, known as the "father of baseball," who invented the scoring system used today.

The greatest scoring feat accomplished by a baseball team in one day took place on October 20, 1865, when the Philadelphia Athletics defeated Williamsburg 100 to 8 in the morning, and that afternoon licked the Danville team of Pennsylvania by the score of 162 to 11.

Joe McCarthy, the only manager in history who piloted teams to pennants in both major leagues, and who created the most successful managerial winning record when he masterminded the New York Yankees to 8 pennants and 7 world-series championships, couldn't even make the big leagues as a player.

Ironically enough, the legendary soldier, General Abner Doubleday, to whom has been ascribed the invention of the game of baseball, is not one of the immortals in Baseball's Hall of Fame at Cooperstown.

A baseball club once was actually expelled from its league because of a dispute over beer. In 1881, Cincinnati, a charter member of the National League, was expelled when the club refused to cease the practice of selling beer in the stands.

A notation appearing on the first score card in baseball reveals that a player named Davis was the first to be fined. He had to pay 6 cents for swearing.

The three famous baseball players for whom dramatic plays were especially written, were Adrian "Cap" Anson, who starred in a play called *A Runaway Colt,* Rube Waddell who starred in *The Stain of Guilt,* and Mike Kelly who starred in *A Rag Baby.*

Larry MacPhail, while boss of the Cincinnati Reds in 1935, originated night baseball played under lights in the major leagues. It was he who, as an American soldier during World War I, won world-wide headline fame for a daring but foolhardy feat when he tried to kidnap the German Kaiser. He almost succeeded.

The Brooklyn Dodgers were once nicknamed "The Bridegrooms" because the married men on the roster outnumbered the single men.

Back in 1890, when the Pittsburgh club lost the astounding total of 113 games out of 136 played, they were nicknamed "The Innocents." However, that label didn't stick because the owners became so adept at stealing players from other teams that the club gained a new nickname—"The Pirates." Ever since, they have been known as the Pittsburgh Pirates.

The lowest number a baseball player ever wore was on the back of the uniform of the clowning pitcher, "Bobo" Newsom. His numeral was "00."

It was the once famous player-manager Patsy Tebeau, of the old Cleveland Spiders, who originated the vicious practice of "spiking." Before games he would have his players sharpen their spikes with files.

The first professional team, the Cincinnati Red Stockings, had a ten-man payroll of $9,300. The star of the team, George Wright, who played shortstop, received $1,400 per season.

The immortal Fred Clarke of the Pittsburgh Pirates was the first outfielder to wear sunglasses.

Roger Bresnahan, one of baseball's greatest catchers, was the player who invented and introduced shin guards for backstops during the 1907 season.

In 1940 in Cuba, Venezuela's best baseball team played the best team from Santo Domingo for the Latin-American championship. Venezuela won on an umpire's close decision. That game aroused such ill feeling between the citizens of the two countries that it almost started a war between Venezuela and Santo Domingo.

The greatest two-fisted fighter in baseball history was George Magerkurth who, before putting in his nineteen years as a major-league umpire, was a heavyweight fighter who had 67 professional bouts in the ring.

From 1886 to 1895 Billy Earle, probably the best catcher in baseball at the time, was forced to play with thirteen different teams in nine years because he was a hypnotist, and his teammates feared the power of his evil eye.

The first night game ever staged in baseball was played in Fort Wayne, Indiana, on June 2, 1883. The game lasted only 7 innings when the lights burned out.

Whiskers were the rule rather than the exception among the game's early players. The last known athlete to appear in the big leagues sporting a beard

was John Titus, who, in 1905, was the outfielder for the Philadelphia Phillies. The only big-league manager in history who wore a full-grown long beard was Gustavus Heinrich Schmelz, pilot of the Cincinnati club in the '80's.

The size of the baseball has not been changed since 1872. It weighs 5 to 5¼ ounces and is from 9 to 9¼ inches in circumference.

The first song about baseball was written in 1867, nine years before the National League was founded.

It was called, "The Baseball Polka" and it was dedicated to the first professional team, the Cincinnati Red Stockings. Down through the years, there were many other songs composed about the game of baseball. Some of the more popular ones were "Catch It on the Fly," "The Day I Played Baseball," "McGuffin's Home Run," "Silver Bat March," "They All Know Cobb," and "That Baseball Rag." Even the world-famed band leader, John Philip Sousa, composed a tune called "The National Game." There was even a song written in honor of baseball club owners. It was called "Magnate's March." A song was composed in honor of umpires. It was called "Let's Get the Umpire's Goat." However, "Take Me Out to the Ball Game" was the greatest song ever written about baseball, and it has outlived all other diamond ballads.

Probably the most traded baseball player in history was Dixie Walker, who, before he became famous as a Brooklyn Dodger outfielder, played with thirteen different minor-league clubs in fourteen years. But a more amazing wanderer was "Honest John" McCloskey who, during his lifetime, managed forty-seven different baseball teams.

The Excelsiors of Brooklyn, forerunners of the Brooklyn Dodgers, was the first professional team to travel from city to city for games.

The first real home-run king of professional base-ball was George Wright, the first high-paid professional. In 52 games he hit an amazing total of 57 home runs.

When the eccentric club owner, Chris Von Der Ahe, couldn't buy a certain bush-league pitcher he wanted for his St. Louis Browns, he bought the entire ball club of twelve men just to acquire the man he wanted.

There was actually a time when the great Ty Cobb was forced to warm the dugout bench even though he was hitting .392. He was the player-manager of the Detroit Tigers, but he kept himself out of the line-up rather than break up an outfield combination which consisted of Heinie Manush hitting .402, Bob Fothergill hitting .406, and Harry Heilman hitting .410.

When the Red Sox fired their infielder Brown, he turned to acting and became the world-famous motion-picture comedian, Joe E. Brown. Also, when the Brooklyn Dodgers turned down a rookie named Merrill, he turned to singing and became the famous singing star of the Metropolitan Opera—Robert Merrill.

As far back as 1874, big-league ballplayers went on a world tour. A team from Boston and the Philadelphia Athletics played fifteen games in England and Ireland.

John Hans Lobert was perhaps the fastest ball-player who ever starred in the major leagues. He was so fleet of foot that once he gave an exhibition racing around the bases against a horse. He won.

The baseball player who made the greatest financial success after his playing days were over was Ty Cobb. His fortune is now estimated at close to $7,000,000.

The most illiterate appraisal of a baseball player, which curiously enough became the most famous scout report in baseball history, was the message sent by the once-famous catcher, Mike Gonzales, to a club owner who was interested in a particular prospect. The odd message which Mike Gonzales sent read: "Good field, no hit." Ironically, the player about whom that famed message was written was catcher Moe Berg, the most highly educated ball-player ever to play in the major leagues.

A baseball was once sold for $1,000,000. It had been autographed by the legendary pitcher, Christy Mathewson, and it was auctioned off at a bond drive during World War I.

It's lucky to be a Yankee! Since 1921 when the New York Yankees won their first pennant, the various players of that club have split an amazing total of $3,315,808.46 in world-series bonuses. And no player in baseball history has received more in world-series "booty" than Frank Crosetti, who, in his nineteen years as a Yankee player and coach, has received close to $70,000 in excess of his regular pay.

The first holdout in big-league baseball was a pitcher named Jim McCormick. In 1887 he held out for a salary of $4,500 for the season. But the Chicago club refused to meet his demands. Jim McCormick remained a holdout for the rest of his life. He quit the game and went into business.

Jim Thorpe is the only baseball player in history who, in a single game, hit three home runs into three different states. In an exhibition game played in a Texas border-town ball park the amazing Indian, then an outfielder for the New York Giants, hit his first home run over the left-field fence into the state of Oklahoma, another over the right-field fence into the state of Arkansas, and his third inside the park in the state of Texas.

The Harvard-bred Eddie Grant, famous third baseman of the New York Giants, was the only major-league player killed fighting in World War I.

Bucky Harris was the only baseball player in history whose wedding was graced by the presence of a President of the United States.

## 118